DRIFTS AND DYNAMICS

Russia's Ukraine War and Northeast Asia

DRIFTS AND DYNAMICS

Russia's Ukraine War and Northeast Asia

Editors

Sriparna Pathak

Manoj Kumar Panigrahi

PENTAGON PRESS LLP

Drifts and Dynamics: Russia's Ukraine War and Northeast Asia

Editors: Sriparna Pathak andManoj Kumar Panigrahi

First Published in 2022

ISBN 978-93-90095-64-3

Published by
PENTAGON PRESS LLP
206, Peacock Lane, Shahpur Jat
New Delhi-110049
Phones: 011-64706243, 26491568
Telefax: 011-26490600
email: rajan@pentagonpress.in
website: www.pentagonpress.in

Printed at Aegean Offset Printers, Greater Noida, U.P.

Dedicated
to
all the people who have lost their loved ones
in conflicts

Contents

Foreword

Russian invasion of Ukraine had unleashed several tectonic changes not only in the European theatre but also in the rest of the world, including in the Northeast Asian region. The initial objectives of Russia, viz., insistence on Ukraine neutrality, no to NATO expansion, no to NATO deployment of missile systems in Russian periphery and "demilitarise" and denazify" Ukraine domestic politics have not been fulfilled so far resulting in the prolonged conflict for several months.

The continuing conflict, besides taking a heavy toll of humans, property and several million homeless migrants, has raised serious questions about the viability and legitimacy of several leaderships' strategic goals and responsibilities. For instance, the Russian "special military operation" – not yet a war according to Russia – indicated to strategic miscalculations, stalemate and had no exit strategy. On the other hand, Ukraine has not been able to mount unbearable costs on Russia, despite the trickling of some aid from the western countries. Thus, the conflict has blurred strategic signalling with no clear red lines, despite claims and counter-claims by the warring parties.

The conflict as such had exhibited three new surprises in warfare preparations with massive bottlenecks in logistics build-up, national mobilisation and drone warfare, even though the initial Russian threat of use of nuclear weapons fortunately did not realise.

Most significantly, the contagion of war had spread to the nook and corner of the world with high energy prices, food prices triggering massive inflation across the board and to prospects of recession. With sanctions, decoupling processes and tariff wars, the Russia-Ukraine conflict is threatening to engulf the whole world.

Also, Russia's invasion of Ukraine is shaping and building narratives in cyber, information warfare and psychological warfare, spilling over into print and electronic media and social networking sites across the globe. The conflict in Ukraine suggests that winning narrative warfare has become as important as kinetic warfare recently.

In this context, it is gratifying to note that the contributors to this volume, mostly young scholars specialising in respective areas of research, offer a timely, relevant and professional assessment on the ongoing conflict.

The focus of the contributors to this volume is on the impact of the events in Ukraine on Northeast Asia – a region that has become well-known for higher economic growth rates, technological transformation but also to the acute territorial integrity and sovereignty claims and counter-claims and the then superpowers interferences. As in the Russia-Ukraine conflict, irredentist claims are rampant in this part of the world. It had also exhibited traditional and non-traditional security challenges for decades.

Russia-China "strategic partnership" since June 2001 has been one of the emerging equations in the region with consequences for regional and international orders, global governance, energy, military, cyber and other domains. Very aptly, the contributors to the volume have highlighted the significance and impact of these developments at length and provide for the academic, media, policy maker and the lay reader alike several relevant inputs.

Srikanth Kondapalli
Dean, School of International Studies
Jawaharlal Nehru University

List of Tables and Figures

Tables

Figures

Abbreviations

AI	Artificial Intelligence
ADIZ	Air Defence Identification Zone
APT	Advanced Persistent Threat
AUKUS	Australia, United Kingdom, USA
BRI	Belt and Road Initiative
BRICS	Brazil, Russia, India, China, South Africa
CCP	Chinese Communist Party
CCTV	China Central Television
CGTN	China Global Television Network
CNP	Comprehensive National Power
CPC	Communist Party of China
CPSU	Communist Party of Soviet Union
CSSTA	Cross-Strait Service Trade Agreement
CTS	Chinese Television System
DAC	Development Assistance Committee
DDoS	Distributed Denial of Service
DPP	Democratic Progressive Party
DPRK	Democratic People's Republic of Korea
ECFA	Economic Cooperation Framework Agreement

ESET	Essential Security against Evolving Threats
EU	European Union
FDI	Foreign Direct Investment
GDR	German Democratic Republic
KMT	Kuomintang
KOICA	Korea International Cooperation Agency
IAEA	International Atomic Energy Agency
IISS	International Institute for Strategic Studies
LDP	Liberal Democratic Party
NATO	North Atlantic Treaty Organization
NEA	Northeast Asia
NPT	Treaty on the Non-Proliferation of Nuclear Weapons
NSP	New Southbound Policy
NTBT	Nuclear Test Ban Treaty
OECD	Organization for Economic Cooperation and Development
OSCE	Organization for Security and Co-operation in Europe
OUN	Organization of Ukrainian Nationalists
PLA	People's Liberation Army
PRC	People's Republic of China
PTT	Professional Technology Template
QUAD	Quadrilateral Security Dialogue
RBMK	Reaktorbolshoymoshchnostykanalny
ROC	Republic of China
ROK	Republic of Korea
RT	Russia Today
SCO	Shanghai Cooperation Organization

SIPRI	Stockholm International Peace Research Institute
THAAD	Terminal High Altitude Area Defence
TPOF	Taiwanese Public Opinion Foundation
UK	United Kingdom
USA	United States of America
VVER	water-water energy reactor
UN	United Nations
UNSC	United Nations Security Council
UNHRC	United Nations Human Rights Council
USSR	Union of Soviet Socialist Republics

List of Contributors

Ashu Maan is a recent graduate from the School of International Affairs of O.P. Jindal Global University. While pursuing his Masters in Diplomacy, Law and Business, he wrote a dissertation titled, "The China Challenge: Exploring U.S.-China Rivalry Through Power Transition Theory". Ashu is currently interning at the Institute of Chinese Studies at New Delhi and works on various aspects of China's international relations. He has previously worked at the Centre for Land Warfare Studies in New Delhi. He has previously published in leading national dailies and for think tanks on aspects of foreign policy, defence and public policy. His most recent publication includes a comparison of U.S. policies towards China under the Trump and Biden administrations, respectively. He is currently working on a book on China's prospects in Afghanistan, due to be published by Lambert Academic Publishing. Besides his academic interests, Ashu also has an interest in the food industry and even has three years' experience in running a small business in the industry. He can be reached at 20jsia-amaan@jgu.edu.in

Ashutosh Kumar is a Doctoral Candidate at the Jindal School of International Affairs of O.P. Jindal Global University. He is also a Japanese language instructor at O.P. Jindal Global University. His present study looks at the evolution and genealogy of Japanese theories of international relations. His research focus is motivated by the efforts of non-Western international relations scholars to make the study of international relations more global in nature with an emphasis on the pluralistic methodological tradition.

Ashutosh also works in the capacity of a Crisis Manager at World Risk and Governance (WoRisGo), a geopolitical risk analysis firm. He conducts threat assessments and risk analyses for the regions of South

Asia and East Asia, respectively. His work entails studying travel security risks and client evacuation from stressed areas, facing natural disasters and political unrest. He headed an evacuation team that saved human assets during the October 2021 Chennai floods. He can be reached over email at akumar1@jgu.edu.in

Divyanshu Jindal is a Research Associate at the Centre for Air Power Studies, New Delhi. His current research focuses on India's cyber diplomacy, and cyber geopolitics. His research interests also include India-Russia relations and Russian foreign policy. He was endowed with the O.P. Jindal Global University Outstanding Merit Scholarship and has a Master's degree in Diplomacy, Law, and Business with specialization in economics and foreign policy from O.P. Jindal Global University, Haryana, in 2021. Before this, he worked as a Systems Engineer at Fidelity Investments, Chennai. He graduated from SRM University in 2016 as a Computer Science engineer. He has cleared UGC-NET in International Relations and Area Studies in 2022. His writings have appeared in the Lowy Institute, 9DASHLINE, The Quint, BRICS Information Portal, Eurasia Review, and other online portals. He can be reached on Twitter @JindalDiv, and over email at divyanshujindal32@gmail.com

Dr. Manoj Kumar Panigrahi is currently an Assistant Professor and co-Director of the Centre for Northeast Asia Studies, in Jindal School of International Affairs at O. P. Jindal Global University. He is also a Non-Residential Research Fellow at Taiwan NextGen Foundation, Taipei. He teaches courses on Cross-Strait relations between Taiwan and China, East Asian Politics, Taiwanese History and Politics, and Peacemaking in Ethnic Conflicts. He has received his Doctorate from the Asia-Pacific Studies program at National Chengchi University in Taipei. His research interests include ethnic conflicts, foreign policy, and cultural issues of Indo-Pacific countries. He writes regularly in a bilingual column about Indian culture and issues in Taiwan. Additionally, he has published articles with *Taipei Times*, Air University. He received the Best Scholarship Recipient Student award from Taiwan's Ministry of Education Scholarship (2016-2020) because of his passion for sharing Indian culture at the grassroots level in over 100 schools by delivering more than 300 lectures during his Doctoral studies. His upcoming publication includes mapping of the Libyan Peace Process. He can be reached over email at mkpanigrahi@jgu.edu.in

Nishant Dilip Sharma is a Doctoral fellow at the Jindal School of International Affairs of O. P. Jindal Global University. He also serves as a visiting researcher at the Institute of Chinese Studies, New Delhi. His research interests include China's domestic governance and the role of China's historical memory in public diplomacy. He has also worked on an archival research project funded by the Indian Council of Social Science Research on Colonial India's Border Making Project vis-à-vis China (1890-1947).

He completed his Masters in International Studies from Christ University, Bangalore, in 2020. Subsequently, he worked as an academic coordinator and political science faculty at Sanjay Ghodawat International School. Being a graduate in Journalism, he has previously served as an opinion writer and panellist for Indian folk, content manager at Capital Via Global Research, and a news writer for NewsTrack live Infomedia. He holds a UGC-NET qualification in International and Area Studies. He can be reached on twitter @NDilipSharma and over email at nsharma@jgu.edu.in

Palak Maheshwari is a postgraduate student of Diplomacy, Law and Business at the Jindal School of International Affairs. While in the final semester of her Masters degree, she undertook an independent research study titled 'Role of Public Diplomacy in Strengthening Asian Cooperation: The Case of Taiwan's New Southbound Policy and South Korea's New Southern Policy in India.' Her research interests include public diplomacy, soft power, East Asia, transnational popular culture, middle power diplomacy, and film/visual cultures. She serves as Coordinator, Centre for Northeast Asian Studies at O.P. Jindal Global University and was awarded for her contribution to institution-building by the Dean of the School of International Affairs. She received a BA (Hons) in Multimedia and Mass Communication from Indraprastha College for Women, University of Delhi, in 2019 and spent some time as a digital journalist with Times Internet before embarking on her postgraduate studies. She is an avid inter-culturalist with a deep interest in language and literature. She is fluent in English and Hindi, and an enthusiastic learner of Korean and Spanish. She can be reached at 20jsia-palak@jgu.edu.in

Dr. Sriparna Pathak is an Associate Professor and former Assistant Academic Dean in the Jindal School of International Affairs of O.P. Jindal Global University, Haryana, India. She is also the founding director of the Centre for Northeast Asian Studies at the School. She teaches courses on Foreign Policy of China as well as Theories of International Relations.

Her previous work experience covers universities like Gauhati University, Don Bosco University; the Ministry of External Affairs, where she worked as a Consultant for the Policy Planning and Research Division, working on China's domestic and foreign policies; think tanks like Observer Research Foundation in New Delhi and Kolkata, respectively, South Asia Democratic Forum in Brussels where she is a Research Fellow and the Centre for Armed Forces Historical Research in New Delhi where she worked as a researcher.

Awarded a Doctorate from the Centre for East Asian Studies, Jawaharlal Nehru University (JNU), Dr. Pathak is fluent in English, Mandarin and Indian languages like Hindi, Bengali and Assamese. She has been a recipient of the joint fellowship awarded by the Ministry of Human Resources Development, India, and the China Scholarship Council, Government of the People's Republic of China, and spent two years in China, actively researching various aspects of China's domestic economy. She has travelled widely in China and her insights on various aspects of China rely heavily on her first-hand experiences there. Her areas of interest are China's domestic economy, trade and economic relations between India and China and China's foreign policy and economic linkages with the world. She is currently working on a project on India's Act East Policy and China's responses. She has been a resource person for various media organisations, colleges, universities and think tanks within India and abroad. She can be reached at @Sriparnapathak on Twitter and over email at sriparnapathak@gmail.com

Sukanya Bali is a Doctoral Scholar at the Jindal School of International Affairs. Her current research focuses on China's Belt and Road Initiative in the Indo-Pacific region. Her interest areas include China's science and technology, human rights, and China's soft-power expansion in the 21st century. Previously, she has worked as a Research Associate at the National Institute of Advanced Studies, IISc, Bangalore. She has published research articles on China's crackdown upon its the giants, tracing the evolution of QUAD over the last two decades and Thailand's new abortion laws among a list of articles. She has also been a resource person for portals like Global Politics, Conflict Reader, The Diplomatist and the South Asia Monitor. She has worked on the Balochistan database on sectarian violence as a project under the international strategic and security studies programme. Ms. Bali has been a research associate for the BRICS Young Scientist Forum, which was a project by the Department of Science and Technology and National Institute of Advanced Studies (NIAS). She can be reached over email at sbali@jgu.edu.in

Introduction

The horrors of the Second World War shook humanity to the core. People and nations across the globe came together to think of plausible ways to avoid a conflict in the future on such a massive scale. As a result, several institutions were created to uphold the peace and stability of the international order. However, as stated by Thomas Hobbes, given that human nature is "nasty, brutish, and short", conflicts emerged.[1] Owing to newly formed laws, treaties, agreements and institutions, the world could keep conflict of the scale of the Second World War at bay. What nevertheless emerged and had all the potential of unleashing conflict on the same scale as of the Second World War was the Cold War between the United States of America (USA) and the Soviet Union.

Several parts of the world emerged as theatres of proxy wars between the two superpowers. Nevertheless, the scale remained relatively limited. What also emerged were several newer types of conflicts, such as economic conflicts and ethnic conflicts, among a long list of others. Given the changing nature of international politics, several paradigms of international relations have also undergone a sea change. An example of this was that economic power also came to be regarded as an essential component of what was hitherto understood as hard power.

In the immediate aftermath of the Second World War, it was often understood that the coercive power of international political relations was limited only to the use of military force. In the words of Joseph Nye (1990), hard power resources are usually associated with command behaviour.[2] However, as countries started transitioning from the realist school of international politics, which focuses primarily on conflict as a focal point, to the liberal school of international politics, states saw economics as an essential facet. The liberal school of international relations holds that states will choose to cooperate rather than go to war to keep their national interests intact.

Given that the forces of globalisation were increasing engagements between states in the form of international trade and investments, states chose to secure their national interests by engaging in business with each other. However, this opened up another opportunity for states to engage in coercive behaviour, and this was through economic sanctions or the more covert use of trade as a weapon to punish others. Irrespective of these changes, the fact remained that a war on the scale of the Second World War had been avoided.

The fall of the Berlin Wall in 1989 and the subsequent collapse of the Soviet Union in 1991 meant that the international system now had only one superpower and the so-called ideological struggle between the superpowers, which was the core of the Cold War, no longer existed! Yet, the nature of world politics, constantly changing now, also saw hitherto less powerful states like China, India, South Korea and Japan, among others, emerge, and play leading roles in international politics. As stated by Nye (1990), the USA became less potent at the end of the 20th century than in 1945.[3] Its share of global products declined from the 1980s onwards. The war had strengthened the USA, but as other countries regained their economic clout, its preponderance started getting eroded,[4]

Most hitherto less powerful countries, which now pushed their way to more power in international politics, did so owing to their rapid economic growth rates. As a result, the system that emerged started by being called a multilateral one with several poles of power. The Northeast Asian region of the world comprised of the countries of the People's Republic of China (PRC), Japan, South Korea, North Korea and Taiwan,[5] became a region to reckon with in international politics.

The Cold War lived on in the division of the Korean peninsula, and North Korea's nuclearization and aggression, aided by the PRC and Russia, became one of the central points of concern. Each of these countries, unique in its ways, presented a new challenge to the existing paradigm of international politics. The PRC's economic rise leading to its political clout in international relations resulting in myriad challenges became another central concern in international politics. Japan, with a pacifist Constitution after the Second World War, emerged as a technological hub. However, given the PRC's wariness concerning a powerful Japan and increasing Chinese aggression in disputed territories, the conflict remained a focal point in Northeast Asia.

South Korea also had astounding economic growth rates in the early 20th century and carved out a niche in international politics. South Korea also leveraged a hitherto unknown facet of power—that of soft power to its advantage and further leveraged its importance in international politics. Taiwan, which the PRC continued to claim to be a part of its sovereign territory, had its share of struggles in international politics as it kept vying for recognition as a separate sovereign state. Against this backdrop, the PRC unleashed a new form of diplomacy called chequebook diplomacy, which ensured that states switched their recognition of Taiwan as a separate state and instead, considered it a part of the PRC.

Chequebook diplomacy, again relying on economics as opposed to the usage of military power, showed how crucial economic clout now was. This form of diplomacy sees financial aid and investment used to curry diplomatic favour. Even though this form of diplomacy emerged and existed from the 1970s onwards in the Pacific Islands region, as the PRC and Taiwan engaged in an arduous process of "buying" recognition from the Pacific nations, this form of diplomacy extends right into the current world order characterised by a pandemic with origins in the PRC. The PRC has extended substantial support to Pacific nations to tackle the COVID-19 pandemic and has leveraged favour of these nations.[6]

While the USA's own foreign policy calculations and specific aspects of its overall power have changed over the years, the fact remains that it is the most powerful nation in the existing international system. To ensure it controls the reins of power, its engagements across the globe continued after 1945, after 1991 and up to now. It was assumed that in the system that emerged after the collapse of the Soviet Union, China would be the primary challenger to the USA. But Russia shocked the world on 24 February 2022 when it unleashed full-scale aggression against Ukraine on the pretext that the North Atlantic Treaty Organization (NATO) forces were expanding eastwards and threatening Russian sovereignty.

Owing to this threat perception of Russian President Vladimir Putin, Russia unleashed the most significant armed invasion in Europe since the Second World War. Thousands of people have died, and towns and cities such as Mariupol in Ukraine lie in ruins. Almost 13 million people, till May 2022, were reported to have been displaced.[7] With this, the once unimagined fears of a third World War have started gaining traction. Countries across the globe have had varied stances on Russia's invasion of Ukraine based on their national interest calculations.

The highly dynamic region of Northeast Asia also has seen varied responses from the states within. The PRC has tried maintaining diplomatic ambiguity and has abstained from various United Nations (UN) resolutions condemning Russia. However, within China, multiple forms of media, including state-sponsored press and social media handles, openly proclaim the West led by the USA as an aggressor and Russia under Putin as a brave hero taking upon a hegemonic West. On the other hand, Taiwan joined the West-led sanctions and resolutions against Russia.

Since the beginning of the war, North Korea has been one of the five countries to support Putin by opposing UN resolutions condemning Russia for the invasion. Pyongyang also blamed the USA as the "root cause of the Ukraine crisis".[8] In this context, North Korea shares 17.3 kilometres of land border and 22.1 kilometres of maritime boundary with Russia.[9] North Korea's nuclear programme has received massive support from the Soviet Union and Russia. Pyongyang expects military technologies and economic aid from Russia in return for its political support. Russia could also leverage its prowess as a permanent member of the UN Security Council (UNSC) to support Pyongyang's nuclear tests. Amidst the unfurling crisis in Ukraine, North Korea has only been conducting more atomic tests. On 5 June 2022, it launched eight ballistic missiles across the country. As stated by Sung Kim, the US special representative for North Korea, the launch is the most ever in a single day![10] In 2022, Pyongyang launched 31 missiles, surpassing its previous record of 2019.[11] North Korea's response to Russia's invasion of Ukraine contrasts with Taiwan's.

One of the few other countries in Northeast Asia, the response of which has been similar to that of Taiwan, is South Korea. At the UN, Seoul voted to condemn the Russian invasion of Ukraine and suspend Russia's membership in the United Nations Human Rights Council (UNHRC). It also upped its pledge for humanitarian assistance to USD 40 million.[12] Some facts in this context include that South Korea has had a long military alliance with the USA and has helped Washington in the Vietnam War and the Iraq War.[13] In 2009, former US president Barack

Obama called South Korea one of America's closest allies and greatest friends.[14] Seoul is also designated as one of the USA's non-NATO allies.

Despite the stance Seoul took against Russia, it was also confirmed that its initial response to the war was very measured. The former government under Moon Jae-in supported international sanctions against Russia as a form of coercive diplomacy. Still, it did not go ahead like some other allies of the USA (like Australia) and impose its sanctions. Some members of the ruling Democratic Party of Korea even blamed Ukraine President Volodymyr Zelenesky for provoking Russia.[15] After further deliberations, Seoul decided to ban direct exports of strategic materials to Russia and Belarus. These included semiconductors. The change between Seoul's initial and current stances deserves a closer look, and the reasons for the shift include Seoul's calculations of its national interests.

On the one hand, it is an essential ally of the USA; on the other, it relies extensively upon the PRC for trade and investment. While the PRC maintains diplomatic ambiguity, Seoul understands how Russia and China want an alternative world order characterised by the demise of US leadership. If such a world order existed, Seoul would have to ensure it treads carefully. Thus, the initial South Korean response to this crisis, which in several quarters is seen as a conflict between Russia and the West, was cautious.

Japan's response to Russia's invasion has been outright condemnation, and Japan, in addition to multilateral sanctions against Russia, has even levied its sanctions against Russia. In fact, in the wake of Russia's invasion of Ukraine, Japan has shifted to a more assertive foreign policy. Japanese Prime Minister Fumio Kishida has stated how Japan has deep stakes in global rules-based order.[16] Japan has also offered financial, humanitarian, and material aid to Ukraine. Japan's response to the crisis also needs a closer study, as it marks novel aspects of diplomacy that did not exist in the era surrounding the Second World War. During the Shinzo Abe administration, Japan sought to engage Russia to find a solution to its bilateral dispute with Russia over the Russian-held Southern Kuril Islands, or what is known as the Northern Territories in Japan. The approach to engage Russia was also to keep Russia from getting further strategically close to the PRC.[17] However, given that Russia has shown its complete disregard for talks or negotiations and unleashed full-scale aggression, Japan has also rethought its foreign policy.

The Japanese Ministry of Foreign Affairs' 2022 Diplomatic Bluebook describes the Northern Territories as "illegally occupied by Russia".[18] Japan has also stated how it will come to Taiwan's defence if the PRC, trying to take advantage of the current situation, attacks Taipei. This statement is much more direct than even what the USA has stated so far on Taiwan. The US policy on Taiwan has, at best, been wishy-washy without clarity. It is precisely because of the lack of certainty about whether or not the USA will come to Taiwan's rescue. Taiwan has started increasing its military responses, and more people in Taiwan think that the USA would steer clear if the PRC were to attack Taiwan militarily.

In an opinion poll published in March 2022 by the Taiwanese Public Opinion Foundation (TPOF), 34.5 per cent of respondents in Taiwan believed that US forces would take part in a joint defence of Taiwan against a Chinese invasion, while 55.9 per cent believed the opposite.[19] Sixty-five per cent of the respondents then thought the USA would come to Taiwan's defence if the PRC were to attack.[20] This marked a sharp decline from six months ago when another TPOF survey recorded confidence in an American military response.

The responses of these highly dynamic countries in Northeast Asia become interesting to study because they show varied levels of responses and approaches to tackle changing drifts in international politics. The reactions of even individual countries have been constantly in flux, as shown by South Korea's example or by the PRC's dubious stances on the crisis. This current crisis can usher in further changes in international politics. Needless to state, with changes in international politics, what will also change is the study of it. Newer theories and paradigms will emerge.

This war has also shown how the nature of warfare itself has been changing. While the war was restricted to the battleground during the Second World War, using economic leverages for coercing countries has become part and parcel of international politics. Amidst Russia's Ukraine war, the battlefield has shifted to the digital domain as various forms of cyber-attacks; disinformation, propaganda, and fake news now dominate. A new Cold War is underway as the digital realm approach is to showcase how the Russian form of governance is superior to the American one. Russia's and China's convergence of interests against the West remains potent to a rule-based international order. The unfolding dynamics in

Northeast Asia, ranging from the fears in Taiwan of a Chinese attack to Japan's bolder stances against China and Russia to North Korea's continued nuclear tests—all become important to study and understand to predict what the future of international politics will look like. In the context of the future of the international political system, the evolving axis between China and Russia becomes important to study.

Thus, the first chapter raises the question whether there was collusion between China and Russia in the invasion of Ukraine in 2022. For this purpose, the chapter undertakes an in-depth study of the 4 February statements regarding the no-limits friendship between Russia and China. The chapter further traces the key words used by the two sides and assesses the extent of coordination between them. It also studies China's three-pronged response to the crisis in Ukraine so far in order to understand the ambiguity surrounding the Chinese response.

The second chapter raises the question whether China can emulate the Russian invasion in Taiwan. To answer this question, the chapter explores cross-straits relations and lays out an understanding of how Taiwan, as a small power, has been trying to balance and bandwagon its relationship between the USA and China. The chapter relies on Wu Yu-shan's concept of 'identity and interest', and details how the PRC has more to lose if it tries to use force to forcibly reunify Taiwan with the Chinese mainland.

Amidst the current crisis, as stated previously the battle has moved from the physical battlefield into the cyber domain as well. The third chapter of this book discusses how the future will witness cyber wars, both as a prelude, as well as a parallel phenomenon to the kinetic wars. Taking off from the example of the disinformation campaigns and the propaganda used in the current crisis in Ukraine, the chapter details how cyber warfare will be a completely new domain in international politics, and how it has all the potentials for creating a new regional security dilemma. The chapter argues how the geopolitics in the region of Northeast Asia will be dependent on cyber dependence, cyber strategies, and cyber diplomacy.

While the contours of battle are changing, diplomacy is also undergoing a serious rethink, as has been exemplified by the varied responses from countries across the globe. With the emergence of multilateralism, the role of middle powers also grew. South Korea as an important middle power has been playing an active role in the international relations of the 21st century. However, for South Korea, the middle power status also comes with expectations of taking a firm stand when faced with a conflict of global proportions like the one unfolding in Ukraine now. The fourth chapter of this book analyses South Korea's decision to join Western-led sanctions against Moscow, and how it has been a major departure from its foreign policy in the past. As an export-dependent economy, South Korea has traditionally refused to directly impose sanctions in cases of conflicts. Instead, it has focused on insulating itself economically from the after effects. Even when there were US-led sanctions during Russia's invasion of Crimea in 2014, South Korea abstained in order to maintain economic ties with Moscow. This chapter looks into why this departure took place and what the future contours of South Korean foreign policy could be in this context.

As contrasted with South Korea, North Korea has been an irritant in international politics, seeking to actively thwart the rules based international order. Ever since the crisis in Ukraine started unfolding in February 2022, the world has also witnessed an increasing number of nuclear tests in the Korean peninsula. North Korea's responses to Russia's invasion of Ukraine also become important to understand where the future lines of conflict and cooperation could be drawn between the West and a possible Russia-China-North Korean axis. In this context, the fifth chapter explores the role of North Korea as a buffer state in the wake of the Ukraine war. It further examines if Russia and China will follow a coordinated policy on North Korea and if they will recognize North Korea as a nuclear weapons state.

Amidst the responses from across the globe to the invasion, the Japanese response becomes a particularly interesting one. Japan has had a territorial dispute with Russia, and one of its foreign policy goals has been to ensure that it does not drive Russia further into the arms of China. However, Russia's invasion of Ukraine has set off a new paradigm in Japanese foreign policy as it is not seen that Japan has opted for a more aggressive stance against Russia. In this context, the sixth chapter studies how the invasion of Ukraine and growing geopolitical uncertainty have propelled Tokyo's policymakers to reconsider their strategic and security outlook. The military adventure of Russia has drawn concerns and comparisons to what China may have in mind for Taiwan or the Senkaku islands. In Japan, the public is debating what Ukraine's invasion could mean for the East Asian region, adding a plethora of momentum to Japan's objective of acquiring 'Enemy base strike capability'. This chapter analyses the Kishida administration's diplomatic reaction to the Russian aggression and how Japan stood its ground coming out of its pacifist comfort zone.

Studying the disinformation campaigns by Russia and China more closely, the seventh chapter studies several cyber-attacks that targeted Ukraine's range of critical cyber infrastructures, including civil, military, and government agencies. This chapter argues that the cyber attacks orchestrated on Ukraine's cyber infrastructure are consistent with a "thunder-run" strategy aimed at bewilderment, chaos, and a swift victory over Ukraine. In addition to these attacks targeting real-world capabilities, information war was also employed to legitimize Russian actions and mould domestic perceptions in the countries concerned. Together, they constitute the fourth front actively manoeuvred by Russia and its silent ally—China. The chapter analyses news reports and social media content promulgated by State-affiliated media in Russia and China and attempts to evaluate the intent and efficacy of these undertakings. The chapter posits that cyber warfare and disinformation campaigns were used complementarily to limit the on-ground capacity of Ukraine and legitimize Russian actions, respectively. As compared to the third chapter, the seventh chapter focuses exclusively on Russia and China's cyber warfare and what the tactics have been so far against the backdrop of the crisis in Ukraine.

Given the battle lines currently being drawn between the West and the Russo-Chinese axis, one of the most frequent questions in international politics is whether Cold War 2.0 has emerged, and what the future could look like. The eighth chapter studies three key dynamics of China's relations with Russia and Ukraine. The chapter raises the question of what China's posture in the Russia-Ukraine crisis amid its strong relationship with Moscow is. China has refused to condemn the invasion in the early days and called upon the West to address Moscow's legitimate concerns. Beijing also refers to Russia's invasion as 'a special military operation' and 'the Russia-Ukraine crisis'. The chapter delves into the contours of the relationship between Beijing-Moscow, and Beijing-Ukraine relations, and considers the past, the present, while outlining the future. Amidst the war, a Cold War approach is looming as they align their interests into blocs reminiscent of the Cold War era. The chapter asks what are the implications of such a China-Russia axis for the future of European security and international relations? In Cold War 2.0, China's growth may rise as a looming threat in the 21st century with a fear of axes of power being formed.

This book came up after about a decade of teaching international politics and Chinese foreign policy, with many contributors to this book writing, publishing and teaching various aspects of international politics. The contributors to this book have all been associated with the Centre for Northeast Asian Studies of O. P. Jindal Global University, Haryana. All of them have spent considerable time in pondering over the subjects of this volume. In fact, all of them were selected for this book given their passion in their designated specialisations in various regions of Northeast Asia. The scholars contributing to this book have been closely monitoring domestic developments in the various countries of Northeast Asia, to understand what the future holds. In contributing to this book, none of the scholars received any funding from abroad or from within India. All chapters are based on open source information. The moral right of each contributor over their respective chapters is asserted.

ENDNOTES

1. Mirriam, Charles Edward., 'Proceedings of the American Political Science Association', Vol. 3, Third Annual Meeting (1906), pp. 151-157.
2. Nye, Joseph S., 'The Changing Nature of World Power', *Political Science Quarterly*, 105 (2), 1990, pp. 177-192.
3. Nye, Joseph S., 'Foreign Policy', *Twentieth Anniversary*, Autumn, No. 80, 1990, pp. 153-171.
4. Ibid.
5. Officially known as Republic of China (ROC)
6. Euan Moyle and Alexandre Dyant, "Chequebook diplomacy in the Pacific: Not just the big fish", *Lowy Interpreter*, 30 June 2020 at https://www.lowyinstitute.org/the-interpreter/chequebook-diplomacy-pacific-not-just-big-fish
7. Paul Kirkby, "Why has Russia invaded Ukraine and what does Putin want?", BBC, 9 May 2022 at https://www.bbc.com/news/world-europe-56720589
8. Sangsoo Lee and Charlotte Bischke, "What North Korea Thinks About the Russia-Ukraine War" Stimson, 10 May 2022, at https://www.38north.org/2022/05/what-north-korea-thinks-about-the-russia-ukraine-war/
9. Wayback Machine, "Neighbouring Countries", (Сопредельные страны) at https://web.archive.org/web/20150708073853/http://www.rosgranitsa.ru/ru/activity/international/countries
10. Sounak Mukhopadhyay, "Nuclear Test by North Korea 'any time': US Envoy", *Livemint*, 8 June 2022 at https://www.livemint.com/news/world/nuclear-test-by-north-korea-any-time-us-envoy-11654656997957.html
11. Sung Kim, "U.S. Special Representative to the Democratic People's Republic of Korea Sung Kim On Recent DPRK Missile Launches", US Department of State,

June 7, 2022 at https://www.state.gov/u-s-special-representative-to-the-democratic-peoples-republic-of-korea-sung-kim-on-recent-dprk-missile-launches/#:~:text=North%20Korea%20has%20now%20launched,And%20it's%20only%20June.

12. Yonhap News Agency, "S. Korean FM joins NATO meeting on Ukraine, reaffirms support for Ukraine", 8 April 2022 at https://en.yna.co.kr/view/AEN20220408002300325
13. Samuel Len, "South Korea Approves 3000 Troops for Iraq", *New York Times*, 4 February 2004 at https://www.nytimes.com/2004/02/14/news/south-korea-approves-3000-troops-for-iraq.html
14. David McKeeby, "President Obama Vows Strengthened U.S.-South Korea Ties", Embassy of the United States in Seoul, 2 April 2009 at https://web.archive.org/web/20090704211009/http://seoul.usembassy.gov/rok_040209.html
15. *Korea Herald*, "Terrible Logic", 2 March 2022 at http://www.koreaherald.com/view.php?ud=20220301000260
16. Sheila A. Smith, "Tokyo Condemns Putin's War, Aids Ukraine", Council on Foreign Relations, 8 March 2022 at https://www.cfr.org/blog/tokyo-condemns-putins-war-aids-ukraine
17. Mercy A. Kuo, "Ukraine War: The Impact on Japan-Russia Relations", *The Diplomat*, 16 May 2022 at https://thediplomat.com/2022/05/ukraine-war-the-impact-on-japan-russia-relations/
18. Victor Lin, "What the 2022 Diplomatic Blue Book Reveals About Japan's Taiwan Policy", *The Diplomat*, 4 May 2022 at https://thediplomat.com/2022/05/what-the-2022-diplomatic-blue-book-reveals-about-japans-taiwan-policy/
19. John Feng, "Taiwan Losing Faith in U.S. Rescue if China Invades—Poll", 23 March 2022, *Newsweek* at https://www.newsweek.com/taiwan-public-opinion-poll-us-military-response-china-invasion-1690831
20. Ibid.

CHAPTER 1

The "No Limits" Friendship: China and Russia amidst the Ukraine Crisis

Sriparna Pathak

ABSTRACT

Russia's invasion of Ukraine has shocked the globe and has the potential to completely reshape the international order. Nevertheless, multilateralism remains the order of the current international system, and countries have been trying to leverage various forms of multilateralism to resolve the conflict. Amidst the unfurling crisis, countries have lobbied against Russian aggression and slapped numerous sanctions against Russia. China, one of the most important poles in the current multilateral international order, however, has refrained from calling out Russia on the devastation it is causing.

A pertinent question in the current context is the extent to which there could be collusion between Russia and China in the current crisis. This question becomes important in order to understand how these two seek to challenge and change the existing international order; to what extent there is an actual collaboration between the two and what the future of the international order could be like if there actually is a complete overhaul of the international system. To understand the extent of the collusion between the two, an in-depth study of the 4 February statements regarding the no-limits friendship between Russia and China becomes important. This chapter traces the key words used by the two sides and assesses the extent of coordination between them.

Certain aspects of China's responses to the Russian invasion of Ukraine are actually in line with the goals of cooperation with Russia as detailed in the 4 February statement. However, some other aspects of the Chinese responses are vague. As such, China's overall response can be viewed through three lenses. The first is that of Chinese diplomacy, in which China maintains a neutral stance, largely abstaining from any vote for or against Russia at the level of international institutions like the United Nations. At the second level, China is actively pushing out propaganda domestically in the Chinese language media (including social media) which supports Russia's actions and tries to draw a parallel between China and Russia and how they have stood up to a hegemonic and exploitative West. At the third level, China tries to keep its relations with Ukraine intact, sending humanitarian and medical supplies. All three of these approaches have underlying reasons. This chapter looks at the ways in which China has been responding to Russia's Ukraine war and discusses reasons behind them. The chapter relies on primary as well as secondary sources from China.

Key words: *China, Russia, Ukraine, war, ambiguity*

Introduction

On 4 February 2022, Russian President Vladimir Putin met his Chinese counterpart, Xi Jinping, at the opening ceremony of the Beijing Winter Olympics. The declaration that followed was that China- Russia friendship had "no limits".[1] The meeting between Putin and Xi was the first face-to-face meeting between the two since 2019. Xi did not travel for meetings with any foreign leader since the COVID-19 pandemic that began in 2020. Thus, beyond the 4 February statement, the fact that Xi chose to meet the Russian leader shows the kind of importance Russia has for China. When Xi Jinping took over the reins of control as the president of the People's Republic of China (PRC) in 2013, it was to Moscow that he had made his first visit. During the visit, the Kremlin had even given Xi a peek into the Russian military's most secretive command and control centre.[2] The depth of the Sino-Russian relationship is reflected in the joint statement that the two had signed in 2001. Signed by Jiang Zemin and Putin, Article 9 of the statement is particularly interesting, as it states that when one of the two contracting parties deems that peace is being threatened or there is a threat of aggression, the two contracting parties will hold consultations to eliminate such threats.[3] This stands in stark contrast to the tumultuous relationship that the Communist Party of China (CPC) had with the Communist Party of the Soviet Union (CPSU) largely until the 1980s.

In 1950, immediately after Mao Zedong proclaimed the "liberation" of the PRC amidst the Cold War, when the world was ideologically divided between the superpowers of the time—the USA and the USSR—Beijing decided it lean to one side, to the side of communism, to the side of the

Soviet Union. The PRC adopted the Soviet model of development and sought the Soviet Union's help to build its nascent industries and to modernise. However, as relations between the two soured during the Sino-Soviet rift, beginning in the late 1950s, the CPC also purged Defence Minister Peng Dehuai in 1959 for being too close to Moscow; accused senior Politburo member Liu Shaoqi of being a "Chinese Krushchev" and accused the party General Secretary, Zhao Ziyang, in 1989 of being the "Chinese Gorbachev" for siding with students in the Tiananmen Square protests.[4] The 2001 statement of friendship between the two slowly set the relations back on track towards normalcy. That statement, extended in 2021, remains an important cornerstone for understanding the Sino-Russian relationship even today.[5] Against this backdrop, it could be assumed that China would support Russia's stance on the eastward expansion of the North Atlantic Treaty Organization (NATO), which remains one of the reasons why Putin launched a full-scale war in Ukraine. However, the fact remains that China neither publicly supports nor denounces Russia's war in Ukraine. Beijing has abstained from voting at the level of the United Nations (UN). Beijing has abstained at the levels of the Security Council as well as the General Assembly on the issue of Russia's war in Ukraine and how it has caused a humanitarian crisis in the Ukraine. When Putin attacked Ukraine in February this year, China refused to call it an 'invasion' and instead blamed the USA and its allies for worsening the situation. Additionally, Chinese state-sponsored media has been consistently calling the war a "special military operation", which is the exact phrase that has been used by Putin.[6] China's response as such has been confusing. Given the 2001 friendship treaty, which was extended just last year in June, along with the 4 February statement between the two sides, the logical expectation would be that China would stand behind Russia hand in hand as a friend in the war in Ukraine. Beijing and Moscow have a common enemy in the West, led by the USA, and Hua Chunyin had even stated in a press briefing in February this year how the USA was "adding fuel to the fire". The two also have a 'multipolar world' campaign that they claim to have launched against the West's 'neo-interventionism' and 'coloured revolutions'.[7] However, China abstained! This points to the peculiarity of the Chinese response to the war. In order to understand how there are divergences between China's and Russia's perceptions of the world, even though the two have a common enemy in the West, it becomes pertinent to the statements released respectively by the two sides post the 4 February meeting between Xi and Putin.

Key points from the Chinese statement on the 4 February meeting

Keeping the current pandemic in mind, the Chinese statement mentioned COVID-19 an ample number of times, stressing how it is pertinent for the globe to stand together against it. While discussing the challenges the current world order faces, the statement also referred to China's commitment to a stable world order, the importance of democracy, the necessity of international fairness and justice and coordination. On the importance of the Sino-Russian relationship, the Chinese statement stressed cooperation, commitment, progress, multilateralism, coordination, mutual support and even the Brazil-Russia-India, China-South Africa (BRICS) grouping.

Based on the number of times the key terms were used in the Chinese statement, Table 1.1 below outlines how many times each term was used.

Table 1.1: Key terms and their usage in the Chinese statement regarding the 4 February meeting between Xi Jinping and Vladimir Putin

Key term	*Usage number*
Cooperation	13
Coordination	7
Mutual support/support	6
(Core) interests	5
COVID-19/pandemic	5
Commitment	3
Progress	3
Multilateralism	2
Democracy	2
BRICS	2

Source: Ministry of Foreign Affairs of the People's Republic of China, 2022.[8]

China has become increasingly aggressive in the pandemic world order and this can be seen in its aggression against multiple countries ranging from India to Vietnam to the Philippines to Taiwan. Its revisionist stance is also seen in its absolute lack of respect for set global norms, be it in the realm of trade or human rights. However, China insists that it is a responsible player, so much so that its diplomats even critique other governments when they try to question the lack of responsibility China shows. This style of aggression in diplomacy is a novel innovation by

China and has been dubbed as 'wolf-warrior' diplomacy. China has also been hostile to all attempts at independent probes into the origins of COVID-19. Given these facets of recent Chinese foreign policy, the usage of the above-mentioned terms in Table 1 become understandable. China tries to portray that it is committed to international peace and stability, which is why it uses terms such as 'commitment' 'multilateralism' and 'coordination' repeatedly. China's rise in the international system has been because of its economic rise, and any instability in the system does not augur well for it. In 2022, China declared that its expected growth rate for the current financial year is 5.5 per cent, which is actually among the lowest since the 1990s! At China's annual parliamentary meeting, while announcing the growth target, Premier Li Keqiang had also stated that China plans to create 11 million new jobs![9] China's growth model has been an export reliant one, any disruption in international trade would mean that China's growth plummets further and unemployment and inflation become worse. Thus, China would want the international system to be stable. Given this reason, the emphasis on 'multilateralism' and 'cooperation' makes sense. China at all costs has avoided taking responsibility for being the origin of the virus, which is why there is a repeated emphasis on a concerted effort to address the pandemic while clearly staying silent on its own responsibility. Because of China's mishandling of the virus when it was first detected in 2019, the world currently stands in the present situation. However, China, while talking of the disruptions the pandemic has caused, stays silent on its own responsibility. In this context, the attempts to move the limelight away from the responsibility or tracing the origins of the virus are seen in the multiple usage of the terms 'COVID-19' and 'pandemic'. China, despite not allowing for political freedoms in its own territory has also talked about 'democracy' in the 4 February statement. In this context, it is also pertinent to point out that China published a White Paper in December last year stating how it is a 'democracy that works'.[10] The attempt here is to state that China's understanding and model of democracy is different from what countries pursuing ideals of Western liberalism understand. In its attempt to portray itself as a responsible player of the international system, it chooses to mention the term 'democracy' at least twice in the 4 February statement. China has constantly stated how it will protect its 'core' interests. In this context, China even came up with its new land border law in November 2021, which took effect from January 2022.[11] Through the enactment of the law, Beijing signals its determination to resolve border disputes on its own preferred terms. The law states that China will "resolutely defend territorial sovereignty and land border security". The tone is clear and upfront that China will safeguard what it calls its "core interests". China's 'core interests' were outlined in a White Paper titled 'China's peaceful development in 2011'.[12] As outlined in it, they include the following:

1. State sovereignty
2. National security
3. Territorial integrity
4. National reunification
5. China's political system and overall social stability
6. Ensuring sustainable economic and social development.

In the years since 2011, China has been more aggressive in safeguarding what it understands as its state sovereignty and territorial integrity, so much so that these 'core interests' even find mention in the 4 February statement.

Signalling the necessity for China and Russia to band together against increasingly difficult situations in the international system ranging from trade wars to supply chain disruptions due to the pandemic, US overtures in the Asia Pacific and the expansion of NATO, among others, the 4 February statement also talked about a fresh vitality to China-Russia relations. It also mentions how the two sides discussed issues of concern around international strategic security and stability. Progress in the bilateral relationship was mentioned along with how the two sides support each other in defending their 'core interests'. The statement also mentions the high-level trust between the two sides. It goes on to outline coordination between them in the Brazil-Russia-India-China-South Africa (BRICS) mechanism.

While China issued the 4 February statement with Russia, emphasising how nothing is beyond the scope of the China-Russia friendship, the fact remains that China was also not aware that Putin would soon after unleash a full-scale attack on Ukraine. There have been US intelligence reports that China asked Russia not to attack Ukraine before the end of the Beijing Winter Olympics.[13] The sporting event ended on February 20 and Putin unleashed a full-scale attack on Ukraine on

February 21. While this correlation does seem to point towards some sort of coordination between Russia and China on the attack, the fact also remains that Beijing did not warn its nearly 6,000 citizens, mostly students and business professionals, to consider leaving Ukraine. The Chinese Embassy in Kiev was struck with the mammoth task of safely evacuating its citizens just as other countries were![14] The question that does come to mind repeatedly is whether Chinese and Russian aims correlate or not in this crisis.

Key points from the Russian statement on the 4 February meeting

In order to lay out an understanding of whether or not coordination existed between China and Russia on Putin's invasion of Ukraine and how they could jointly posture an alternate global governance model amidst the devastation in Ukraine and beyond, it first becomes pertinent to trace the key terms the Russian side has used in outlining the 4 February meeting between Xi and Putin. Russia's statement on the 4 February meeting is much more elaborate than that of the Chinese side. It runs into easily over 5,000 words.[15] Unlike the Chinese statement, which denounces attempts at disrupting international peace, the Russian side actually calls out countries by name and details how it perceives their actions as being contradictory to what it sees as international peace and stability. Table 1.2 outlines the key terms used by the Russian side and indicates how many times they have been used in the statement, in order to indicate their importance for Russia.

Table 1.2: Key terms and their usage in the Russian statement regarding the 4 February meeting between Xi and Putin

Key term	*Usage number*
Development	50
Security	42
Cooperation	41
Democracy/democratic	20
Peace/peaceful	16
Multipolarity/multilateral	15
Pandemic/corona virus/COVID-19	12
Human rights	12
Changes/transformation	11
Shanghai Cooperation Organization (SCO)	9
Power	8

Source: Kremlin, Russia, 4 February 2022.[16]

A closer analysis of the key terms used helps understand the larger foreign policy goals behind the usage. The Russian side stated development multiple times in the context of how China-Russia relations have developed and how development in economic, security, social and cultural terms is the need of the hour in today's international relations. Russia stated how humanity is entering a new phase of rapid development and profound transformation. This indicates two possibilities:

1. Russia and China are steering the world away from the West's hegemony and leading the world into a new type of development. Both are willing to cooperate on problems in the current epoch ranging from climate change to the pandemic and have better strategies than the West.
2. Russia was indicating that after its invasion of Ukraine, international politics would undergo a sea change.

The second possibility seems more plausible given that Russia used the term 'security' the second highest number of times in the statement. Through the usage of the term 'security', Russia indicated how it would adhere steadfastly to what it sees as its legitimate security concerns and protect them against the eastward expansion of the NATO. The usage of the term 42 times, along with China's usage of 'core interests' a relatively high number of times indicates how Russia and China understand each other and are willing to protect each other's security concerns.

In this context, Russia used the term 'cooperation' 41 times, trying to emphasise over and over again how any attack on what China or Russia sees as their security interests respectively may lead to greater solidarity between them and a united front against the aggressor. Both China and Russia, despite being led by dictators, have used the term 'democracy' an ample number of times to showcase how the two understand each other's concepts of governance and how their understanding of 'democracy' is different from that of the liberal world. Moscow states, "There is no one-size-fits-all template to guide countries in establishing democracy. A nation can choose such forms and methods of implementing democracy that would best suit its particular state". This again has two possibilities as the reasons behind the usage.

1. Russia wanted to show China how it understands that Chinese actions in Xinjiang, Tibet and Hong Kong are not to be commented upon by the Western world, since understandings of democracy

are different in China and Russia from that in the West.

2. Russia, planning its invasion in Ukraine, was warning the world how its actions in the bordering areas of Ukraine are actually to help the ethnic groups there and are in fact democratic. Donbas is predominantly Russian-speaking and Russia in the past has repeatedly mentioned "liberating" the rest too.[17]

In its attempt to portray that an alternate model of international relations exists as perceived by Russia and China, respectively, the Russian side in its statement also reiterated 'peace' and 'multilateralism' multiple times. The attempt was to send a warning to the Western states to stop criticising China for its mishandling of the COVID-19 virus, which led the endemic to turn into a global pandemic as well as to showcase that Russia and China, through their efforts in regional organisations like the BRICS and SCO, create multilateralism in the truest sense. Russia even mentioned in the statement how multi-polarity, economic globalisation, the advent of an information society, and transformation of the global governance architecture are pertinent today. The mention of economic globalisation by Russia has two plausible reasons:

1. To showcase how Western countries engaging in trade and tariff wars are disruptive of globalisation and how Russia and China, which reiterate interdependence frequently especially at forums like SCO and BRICS, are true upholders of the current multilateral world order.
2. Russia wanted to indicate that economic sanctions, which it knew would be a definite fallout of its impending invasion of Ukraine, would cause disruptions in the global trading system.

Russia reiterates the SCO multiple times to indicate how Moscow and Beijing truly aim at a more peaceful international system than the West. In its attempts to show how Russian and Chinese models of governance are better than that of the West, Moscow even stated how some "actors representing the minority on the international scale continue to advocate unilateral approaches to addressing international issues and resort to force; how they interfere in the internal affairs of other states, infringing on their legitimate rights and interests, and incite contradictions, differences and confrontation, thus hampering the development and progress of mankind".[18]

It even goes to the extent of calling naming countries for being disruptors of peace in the international system. It mentions how the trilateral security partnership between Australia, the USA and the UK (AUKUS) is a development of concern in international relations, how Japan's plans on the destroyed Fukushima nuclear plant are deeply concerning, how US plans in the Asia-Pacific and in European regions are "risks to international and regional security", how Russia and China through BRICS aim at deepened strategic partnerships and how the SCO aims at enhancing a "polycentric world order".

There are two interesting points of departure between the Chinese and Russian statements:

1. The Russian statement, besides being much lengthier than the Chinese one, is more elaborate and covers many more issues.
2. The Russian statement is more direct and calls out countries by name as being disruptive of international peace. The Chinese side shies away from making direct verbal or stated attacks on other countries of the international system.

What remains interesting about the Russian statement is that it echoes all of China's recent foreign policy statements, be it on COVID-19, or the centrality of regional organisations like BRICS and SCO in today's world, the politicisation of the issue of terrorism, and even the usage of the term 'Asia Pacific' instead of the term 'Indo-Pacific', which has often been criticised by China.[19] In fact, in 2018, China had even mocked Australia over the concept of the Indo-Pacific. Speaking at an annual media conference in Beijing, Chinese Foreign Minister Wang Yi had termed the Australian and the US preference of describing the region as the 'Indo-Pacific' instead of 'Asia-Pacific' as an attention-grabbing idea that would "dissipate like ocean foam".[20] Russia, in its 4 February statement, terms the region as Asia-Pacific' as is preferred by Beijing.

Russia, in its 4 February statement also mentions the intention of the two sides to develop cooperation within the Russia-India-China format. While this was before Russia's invasion of Ukraine, the fact was that China had already attacked and infiltrated across Indian borders during the Galwan clash of 2020, and even after 15 rounds of military corps commander talks between India and China as of March 2022, the situation on the border between India and China was far away from resolution. India's External Affairs Minister, Dr. S. Jaishankar had even spoken about how Chinese military aggression at the borders has adversely impacted India-China relations.[21]

The reason why Russia has used the terms and concepts used by China in its 4 February statement is to signal a united front by Russia and China. While Russia and China have also several points of disjuncture between them, including on how they envisage their roles in Central Asia, views on various issues within the SCO and BRICS, their varying levels of bonhomie with India and Pakistan, respectively, Moscow and Beijing find a large ground for alignment against the West. Both see the West as hegemonic and both want to replace what they call Western hegemony with an alternate model of governance. That being stated, both see their own selves as the sole leader in the international system. However, given the fact that the West led by the USA is still formidable, both find common ground in adopting narratives signalling how an alternative model of international relations as per the governance models of these two countries will be a better option. Despite the fact that Russia and China declared their deep friendship in the 4 February statement, the fact is that on the issue of Russia's invasion of Ukraine, China has adopted a very nuanced strategy, to the extent that it is actually walking a diplomatic tightrope between Russia and the West. China's response to Russia's invasion of Ukraine is actually a three-pronged strategy as shown in Figure 1.1.

Figure 1.1: China's three-pronged response to Russia's invasion of Ukraine

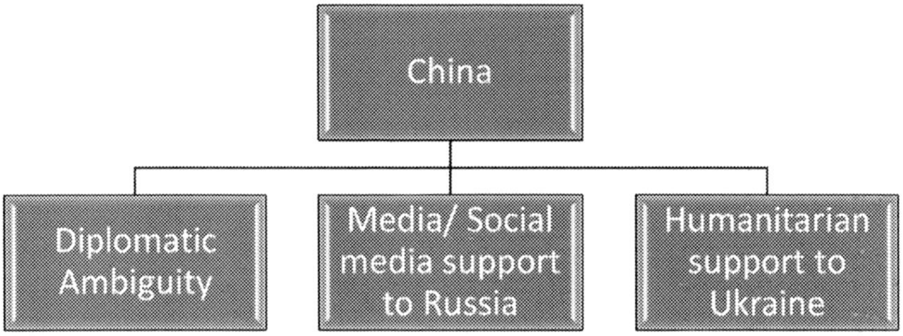

1. Diplomatic Ambiguity: Beijing's diplomatically ambiguous position is reflected most evidently in its votes at the United Nations. China not just abstained but kept up its streak of abstentions at the UN General Assembly. On February 25, when the first instance of voting at the level of the UN took place at the Security Council to condemn Russia's attack of Ukraine, China abstained. It also abstained from a condemnation of the war by 141 countries in the UN General Assembly.

In April this year, when the UN General Assembly adopted a resolution calling for Russia to be suspended from the Human Rights Council, China voted against it. This time it did not abstain! The resolution had a two-third majority of those voting, minus abstentions. Ninety-three countries voted in favour, while 24 voted against it. Russia, China, Cuba, North Korea, Iran and Vietnam voted against the resolution, while abstentions included India, Brazil, South Africa and Mexico, among others.[22] The question here again arises as to why China has abstained on other UN resolutions while voting against this particular resolution for the suspension of Russia from the Human Rights Council. The reasons behind this move by Beijing are two:

1. As revealed by the commonality in the usage of the term 'human rights' and 'democracy' in the 4 February statements from China and Russia (as discussed in the preceding sections), China and Russia hold that their understanding of human rights is different from that of the Western world of liberal democracies. Thus, excluding Russia from the Human Rights Council based on a Western interpretation of what constitutes human rights is not acceptable to China.
2. Walking the diplomatic tight rope between Russia and the West, China at several UN votings abstained on the Ukraine issue. However, it was necessary for Beijing to signal that it will not stop supporting Russia altogether. Hence, at this juncture, Beijing voted against.

China has repeatedly tried to present itself as a responsible player in the international system and has called for a peaceful end to the conflict. It has maintained this particular stance in the multiple official statements it has released on the issue. This particular Chinese stance of showcasing itself as a responsible player calling for peace is best exemplified by the statement of the Chinese Foreign Minister Wang Yi, who, on 31 March 2022 at the First Neighbouring Countries of Afghanistan Plus Afghanistan Foreign Ministers' Dialogue in Tunxi, laid out China's position. He reiterated the necessity for peaceful dialogue, avoiding a Cold-War like mentality and opposing unilateral sanctions imposed by individual countries.[23]

While these statements were made in the context of Afghanistan, they can be applied equally easily in the case of Russia. Even though China has rejected calling the Russian move in Ukraine an invasion, Xi has called for "maximum restraint" and has talked about being pained at seeing the flames of war in Europe. Xi made these remarks at a virtual meeting with French President Emmanuel Macron and German Chancellor Olaf Scholz in March this year and added that these three countries should jointly support peace talks between Russia and Ukraine.[24] In March this year, Chinese Foreign Minister Wang Yi blamed the "Cold War mentality" as the real reason for the war in Ukraine.[25] In February itself, while the USA, EU and their allies stepped up punitive measures against Russia, Beijing stated it was opposed to illegal unilateral sanctions against Moscow and that it would continue to carry out its normal trade cooperation with it.[26] At a regular press briefing in Beijing. Foreign Ministry spokesperson Wang Wenbin stated that China opposes the use of sanctions to solve problems and is even more opposed to unilateral sanctions that have no basis in international law.[27] So, while Wang Yi was calling for a peaceful dialogue outlining how a Cold War mentality is detrimental for peace and how sanctions do not augur well for stability; at the First Neighbouring Countries of Afghanistan Plus Afghanistan Foreign Ministers' Dialogue, he was echoing China's stances even on the issue of Russia's invasion of Ukraine! Diplomatically, China is purposely maintaining ambiguity, abstaining on most votes against Russia at the level of the UN, while emphasising peace and the need for dialogue, talking about how unilateral sanctions are futile for global peace because China needs to project itself as a responsible player while shielding Russia tacitly. It is precisely for this reason that China has not sent weapons to Russia for use in Ukraine, as confirmed by Chinese Ambassador to the USA Qin Gang.[28] US President Joe Biden had warned Xi that there would be consequences if Beijing provided material support to Moscow![29] Also, China cannot openly support Russian aggression, lest it itself falls victim to Western-style sanctions and is painted as a pariah state for its public support of an invading country like Russia!

2. **Chinese Media/Social Media support to Russia.** While China has been purposely diplomatically ambiguous on Russia's invasion of Ukraine, Chinese social media is immensely supportive of Putin and his war in Ukraine. It becomes pertinent to track the discourse on Chinese social media because online discourses and state propaganda offer glimpses

into how Beijing views Russia's invasion of Ukraine. China's state news agencies like Xinhua call the invasion a "special military operation", or at best the "Russia-Ukraine crisis" but never refer to it as an invasion.[30] China's state broadcaster mentioned civilian casualties only three weeks after Russia invaded.[31] State outlets have also liberally promoted the conspiracy theory that the USA is funding the development of biological weapons in Ukraine.[32]

The Russian Defence Ministry, in March this year, released documents that it supposedly acquired from the personnel of a bio lab in Ukraine this year, exposing how the USA and its NATO allies are conducting research on biological weapons in Ukraine. The documents apparently also mention plans for spreading avian flu through migratory birds and pathogens such as bacteria and viruses that can be transmitted from bats to humans.[33] Chinese state media lapped up the propaganda immediately and *Global Times* went to the extent of demanding an answer from the West about its biological warfare.[34] This particular disinformation can actually be placed in the context of the 4 February statements of the two countries. Both have elaborately talked about the COVID-19 pandemic and the Russian statement echoes China's stances on the pandemic. Utilising the opportunity unleashed by Russia's war in Ukraine, the two have stepped up the same kind of attempts seen from China in the past in blaming the USA and a host of other countries for the origin of the pandemic!

Chinese netizens tend to show a sympathy for the Russian position, as the narrative that the USA and the West are to blame for the conflict are increasingly common. Because of the current wave of the pandemic in China and the extremely harsh lockdown, domestic affairs still dominate the news. However, when there is a discussion around Russia, the sense that prevails is that of sympathy, not for Ukraine, but for Russia! The reasons behind this include the state's own narrative, which is pushed out through state-run tabloids like *Global Times*; as well as by the Chinese people's attraction for the character of Putin. As stated by Guo Jinyue of the Ministry of Foreign Affairs' China Institute of International Studies, Putin's personal character satisfies a certain "psychological need" of the Chinese people. Putin, as compared to the solemn and firm appearance that CPC leaders generally have, leaves a brave and energetic impression. Guo adds that Putin's "tough-guy" image fits nicely with the traditional Chinese desire for a powerful leader.[35]

Taiwan-based Doublethink Lab, which is a cyber monitoring group, released a report on how the close relationship between Russian and Chinese state media has helped in amplifying Russian propaganda on Chinese social media platforms like Weibo.[36] As stated in the report, Chinese state media and influential accounts on Weibo have been attempting to build a connection between Putin's claim of "Ukrainian Nazism" with the 2019 protests in Hong Kong against the anti-extradition bill. Weibo and social media have gained so much in importance that the Ukrainian Embassy even issued a statement in Chinese condemning Russia on Weibo. Governments in the USA, the UK, and EU countries, as well as Russia, issued statements on Weibo in response to the war. The battle clearly has moved beyond the battlefield and social media and media usage have become extremely important tools.[37] Meta owned Facebook has even been called out for letting China Global Television Network (CGTN) place advertisements that promote Russian propaganda and disinformation about the war.[38] The advertisements are aimed at audiences in Hong Kong and Central Asian countries.

China's media space is tightly controlled, and Russia's invasion of Ukraine is an opportunity for Beijing to use information warfare and advance its narrative of how the West is against Russia and China. It is precisely because of this that narratives of US high-handedness on Taiwan or its supposed support to protesters in Hong Kong gets entangled with narratives on Russian heroism against the West. While China maintains ambiguity on its actual stance on the war, tracking Chinese media and social media, all of which operate within highly controlled spaces gives an understanding of where China's political compass truly lies on the Russian invasion of Ukraine.

3. Humanitarian Aid and Support to Ukraine: The bilateral relationship between China and Ukraine has undergone several phases of warming and freezing. Given an intensification of economic and trade ties between 1992 and 2004, the bilateral relationship received a fillip.[39] Political relations froze in 2005 as Kiev had allowed a Taiwanese official to visit Ukraine, and relations remained frozen till 2010. In 2010, the two sides signed a Joint Declaration on the Establishment of Strategic Partnership.[40] Nevertheless, since 2014, ever since the Maidan Revolution took place, China has kept a low-key official contact with Ukraine. China considers the Maidan Revolution to be a Western-sponsored action.[41] The year 2022 marks 30 years of establishment of diplomatic relations between the two sides. Amidst Russia's invasion of Ukraine, on March 17, China's Ambassador to Ukraine, Fan Xianrong, stated that China would support Ukraine both politically and economically.[42] In March, China sent its first shipment of humanitarian aid to war-torn Ukraine. Foreign Ministry spokesperson Zhao Lijian stated that the first batch of a five million Yuan or USD 791,300 emergency aid donation was sent from Beijing through the Red Cross Society of China.[43] Zhao added that the food and other necessities were arranged at the request of Ukraine. On 21 March. Wang Wenbin stated that China would provide an additional 10 million Yuan or USD 1.57 million worth of humanitarian assistance to Ukraine.[44] He made the comments at a regular press briefing in Beijing.

In addition to humanitarian aid, what China has also done is that it has stated it will work with the international community to provide "necessary mediation" between Ukraine and Russia when the time is right.[45] Wang Yi, speaking at a press briefing during China's annual legislative meetings in Beijing, had stated that China supports the United Nations in coordinating humanitarian assistance to Ukraine. The question that arises here is why does China seem to signal it cares for Ukraine, while it has repeatedly spoken of the 'no limits friendship' with Russia. The answer is twofold:

1. The invasion gives China a chance to showcase how it truly cares for the lives of civilians caught in conflicts in the way a true leader of the international system should be. This is why China, while shielding Russia from being ousted out of the Human Rights Council of the UN for human rights violations, talks about sending humanitarian supplies to Ukraine. Needless to state, China's stance is completely dubious; if it really cared about rights violations and civilian lives, it would not have voted in favour of Russia when the resolution regarding ousting Russia from the Human Rights Council of the UN was taken up.
2. China relies on Ukraine for a significant portion of its food security. Ukraine is also an important country in China's dream project of the Belt and Road Initiative. It cannot afford to completely alienate Ukraine. In fact, Chinese Ambassador to Ukraine Fan Xianrong had even stated in March to how China is a friendly country for the Ukrainian people and that China will "respect the path chosen by Ukrainians because this is the sovereign right of every nation".[46] The irony is that while China made statements about sovereignty,

Russia with which it has a 'friendship with no limits' deepened its actions to decimate Ukraine's sovereignty!

Conclusion

China's stances on the Russian invasion through their diversities actually signal the difficult spot China finds itself in the current scenario. While Russia and China speak of a "no-limits" friendship, the fact actually is that the two have an ad-hoc arrangement to oppose the West, which both see as their primary competitor in the current international system. China's rise in the international system has been facilitated by its linkages to the international system, utilising the forces of global trade, capital flows, and investment.

For Russia, the case has not been the same, as its economy has largely been stagnating and is not as deeply integrated as the Chinese economy. For Russia, a hedonistic step such as that of invading Ukraine to show its opposition to NATO's expansion and Western hegemony is largely without calculations of how badly Western sanctions could hit the Russian economy. For China, even the secondary impact of the current sanctions will derail its economic growth, which in turn will have larger repercussions for its comprehensive national power (CNP).

CNP or *zongheguoli* (综合国力) is a concept that has been important in the political thought of the PRC since the 1980s. It was first introduced into official documents only in 1992.[47] It measures the general power of a country and is calculated by numerically combining the various quantitative indices to create a single number to measure the power of the country. The indices taken into account include military, political, economic, and cultural factors. China's foreign policy calculations are also to enhance its CNP.

China, since the 19th Party Congress, has been signalling it is ready to take on the leader of the international system. Xi had even stated at the 19th Party Congress in 2017 as to how developing countries can follow the Chinese model of governance that has led China on the road of economic prosperity.[48] While the USA under former President Donald Trump was seen as pulling out of various institutions of multilateralism or threatening to do so, China was emphasising on more multilateralism to showcase how it has now moved away from Deng Xiaoping's policy of keeping a low profile or *taoguangyanghui* (韬光养晦) and is ready to fill the vacuum that will be left behind by the USA's disappearance as the leader of the international system. Before Russia invaded Ukraine in February this year, through the Beijing Winter Olympics, the PRC yet again showcased how it can host large-scale international events of significance and even utilised the games for multiple political events even though the Olympics committee clearly speaks about non-politicisation of sports.

The 4 February statement between Xi and Putin was one of these important political events that took place during the Games, and China, in its attempt to show an alternative model of governance as compared to the West's, signed the "no-limits friendship" with Russia. Given the amorphous nature of international politics and backdoor diplomacy, there can be no guarantee that China actually requested Russia to hold on to the invasion till the Games was over. However, what is definitely a fact is that the Russian statement on the 4 February meeting between Xi and Putin reflects Chinese thinking on how international politics should be! This is reflected in the fact that despite both being dictatorships, they talk about democracy, a just international system, a unified response to COVID-19, with Russia even going to the extent of referring to the Indo-Pacific as Asia Pacific, just the way China has been wanting the world to!

Therefore, there is definitely collusion between Russia and China on trying to orchestrate an alternative model of international relations. Both are revisionist powers seeking to steer the world away from the principles of liberalism and multilateralism, while harping on the terms and utilising narratives to showcase that they want a truly multilateral order. The fact is that as opposed to the Western principles of liberalism or multilateralism, China's world view on international politics is vertical, with China at the top and the other countries below it. It does not follow a horizontal distribution of power as existent principles of multilateralism do.

A derailment of growth rates is not something that China wants, because of which it walks a tight rope, maintaining diplomatic ambiguity on Russia's invasion. It also does not want to completely burn its bridges with Ukraine, which is an important partner for China for food security. It also is an important node in China's ambitious Belt and Road Initiative (BRI). In March this year, amidst the unfolding crisis in Europe, DB Schenker, which is a prominent German third-party logistics provider, announced that it was temporarily suspending land, air and sea transport to and from Russia. Similarly, Hapag-Lloyd had confirmed that it was no longer accepting bookings involving Russia, Belarus, and Ukraine. A statement issued by the inland Port of Duisburg in Germany, a key hub for BRI shipments, noted that international insurers are likely to stop offering coverage for shipments transiting Russia and Belarus.[49] None of these augurs well for China and do not fit into ideal geo-economics for Beijing.

In such a scenario, therefore, Beijing has tried to keep its bridges intact with Kiev, talking about peace, dialogue and restraint on all sides! China's actual political stances can be understood through a closer reading of the narratives it puts out in its domestic media and on its social media sites. The readiness to lap up Russian disinformation to signal how the West is now creating wars in Europe, and then will eventually do so for China (in Hong Kong, Taiwan and beyond in the Indo-Pacific) implies how China leverages the opportunities created by the invasion. As such, China being a transactional state, will try to reduce the spill over of Russian actions at all costs, while leveraging the most out of the opportunities created by it.

ENDNOTES

1. Lingling Wei, "China Declared Its Russia Friendship Had 'No Limits.' It's Having Second Thoughts", *The Wall Street Journal*, 3 March, 2022 at https://www.wsj.com/articles/china-russia-xi-putin-ukraine-war-11646279098
2. Srikanth Kondapalli, "Putin's war has brought Xi factional trouble", *Deccan Herald*, 6 March, 2022 at https://www.deccanherald.com/amp/opinion/putin-s-war-has-brought-xi-factional-trouble-1088425.html?fbclid=IwAR3SZyiHw4xIGnZgpH8eUxVB2judLHhth2GBLxj_00foneK_b2ZZeVUIMSw
3. Ministry of Foreign Affairs of the People's Republic of China, "Treaty of Good-Neighborliness and Friendly Cooperation Between the People's Republic of China and the Russian Federation", 24 July 2001 at https://web.archive.org/web/20110605071535/http://www.fmprc.gov.cn/eng/wjdt/2649/t15771.htm
4. Srikanth Kondapalli, "Putin's war has brought Xi factional trouble", *Deccan Herald*, 6 March, 2022 at https://www.deccanherald.com/amp/opinion/putin-s-war-has-brought-xi-factional-trouble-1088425.html?fbclid=IwAR3SZyiHw4xIGnZgpH8eUxVB2jud LHhth2GBLxj_00foneK_b2ZZeVUIMSw
5. Reuters, "Russia, China extend friendship and cooperation treaty—Kremlin", June 28, 2021 at https://www.reuters.com/world/china/russia-china-extend-friendship-cooperation-treaty-kremlin-2021-06-28/
6. Sutirtho Patranobis, "China refuses to call Russian attack on Ukraine an 'invasion', blames US", *Hindustan Times*, 24 February 2022 at https://www.hindustantimes.com/world-news/china-refuses-to-call-russian-attack-on-ukraine-an-invasion-blames-us-101645700094267.html

7. Srikanth Kondapalli, "Putin's war has brought Xi factional trouble", *Deccan Herald*, 6 March, 2022 at https://www.deccanherald.com/amp/opinion/putin-s-war-has-brought-xi-factional-trouble-1088425.html?fbclid=IwAR3SZyiHw4xIGnZgpH8eUxV B2judLHhth2GBLxj_00foneK_b2ZZeVUIMSw
8. Ministry of Foreign Affairs of the People's Republic of China, "President Xi Jinping Held Talks with Russian President Vladimir Putin", 4 February 2022 at https://www.fmprc.gov.cn/mfa_eng/zxxx_662805/202202/t20220204_10638923.html
9. Evelyn Cheng, "China sets GDP target of 'around 5.5%' for 2022", *CNBC*, 4 March 2022 at https://www.cnbc.com/2022/03/05/china-on-deck-to-reveal-its-2022-gdp-target.html
10. The State Council Information Office of the People's Republic of China, "China: Democracy that Works", 4 December 2022.
11. Shuxian Luo, "China's land border law: A preliminary assessment", Brookings, 4 November 2021 at https://www.brookings.edu/blog/order-from-chaos/2021/11/04/chinas-land-border-law-a-preliminary-assessment/
12. Feng Zhaokui, "What Are China's Core Interests?", China-US Focus, 21 October 2014 at https://www.chinausfocus.com/foreign-policy/what-are-chinas-core-interests-2
13. Katie Bo Lillis and Natasha Bertrand, "China asked Russia to delay Ukraine invasion until after Olympics, Western intel shows", *CNN*, March 3, 2022 at https://edition.cnn.com/2022/03/02/world/china-russia-ukraine-invasion-olympics-western-intel/index.html
14. Shi Jiangtao, "Ukraine invasion: did China know about Putin's plans, or was Beijing tricked?", *South China Morning Post*, 5 March 2022 at https://www.scmp.com/news/china/diplomacy/article/3169246/ukraine-invasion-did-china-known-about-putins-plans-or-was
15. Kremlin, "Joint Statement of the Russian Federation and the People's Republic of China on the International Relations Entering a New Era and the Global Sustainable Development", 4 February 2022 at http://en.kremlin.ru/supplement/5770
16. Ibid.
17. Paul Kirby, "Donbas: Why Russia is trying to capture eastern Ukraine", *BBC*, 26 May 2022 at https://www.bbc.com/news/world-europe-60938544
18. Kremlin, "Joint Statement of the Russian Federation and the People's Republic of China on the International Relations Entering a New Era and the Global Sustainable Development", 4 February 2022 at http://en.kremlin.ru/supplement/5770
19. Stiftung Wissenschaft und Politik, "From Asia Pacific to Indo-Pacific", SWP Research Paper 2020/RP 09, 01.07.2020, 43 Seiten, doi:10.18449/2020RP09 at https://www.swp-berlin.org/10.18449/2020RP09/
20. Bill Birtles, "China mocks Australia over 'Indo-Pacific' concept it says will 'dissipate'", *ABC News*, 8 March 2018 at https://www.abc.net.au/news/2018-03-08/china-mocks-australia-over-indo-pacific-concept/9529548
21. Press Trust of India, "India-China relations going through a 'very difficult phase': Jaishankar", *Business Standard*, 5 May, 2021 at https://www.business-standard.com/article/current-affairs/india-china-relations-going-through-a-very-difficult-phase-jaishankar-121050500854_1.html
22. United Nations, "UN General Assembly votes to suspend Russia from the Human Rights Council", 7 April 2022 at https://news.un.org/en/story/2022/04/1115782
23. Ministry of Foreign Affairs of the People's Republic of China, "Wang Yi Chairs the

First "Neighboring Countries of Afghanistan Plus Afghanistan" Foreign Ministers' Dialogue", 31 March 2022 at https://www.fmprc.gov.cn/mfa_eng/wjb_663304/wjbz_663308/activities_663312/202204/t20220401_10663013.html

24. *Al Jazeera*, "China's Xi: Beijing supports peace talks between Russia, Ukraine", 9 March 2022 at https://www.aljazeera.com/news/2022/3/9/chinas-xi-beijing-supports-peace-talks-between-russia-ukraine
25. DW, "Why China thinks the West is to blame for Russia's war in Ukraine", at https://www.dw.com/en/why-china-thinks-the-west-is-to-blame-for-russias-war-in-ukraine/a-61119517
26. K.J.M. Varma, "China opposes US, EU sanctions against Russia; says will carry out normal trade with Moscow", *The Print*, 28 February 2022 at https://theprint.in/world/china-opposes-us-eu-sanctions-against-russia-says-will-carry-out-normal-trade-with-moscow/852335/
27. Ibid.
28. Agence France Presse, "Amid Flack, China's US Envoy Says Beijing Now Not Sending Arms To Russia", *NDTV*, March 20, 2022 at https://www.ndtv.com/world-news/russia-ukraine-war-amid-flack-chinas-us-envoy-says-beijing-now-not-sending-arms-to-russia-2833082
29. AFP, "China envoy says Beijing not sending arms to Russia, for now", *Wion News*, 21 March 2022 at https://www.wionews.com/world/china-envoy-says-beijing-not-now-sending-arms-to-russia-464309
30. Rachel Cheung, "Russia-Ukraine war: In Chinese media, the US is the villain", *Al Jazeera*, 6 April 2022 at https://www.aljazeera.com/news/2022/4/6/china-media-coverage-ukraine-war
31. Ibid.
32. Own Churchill, "Ukraine bioweapons claim opens new front in China-US tensions", *South China Morning Post*, 10 March 2022 at https://www.scmp.com/news/china/article/3169909/ukraine-bioweapons-claim-opens-new-front-china-us-tensions
33. China Military Online, "US owes world answer on bio lab", 14 March 2022 at http://eng.chinamil.com.cn/view/2022-03/14/content_10140698.htm
34. *Global Times*, "US owes world an answer on bio lab: Global Times editorial", 11 March 2022 at https://www.globaltimes.cn/page/202203/1254649.shtml
35. David Gitter, "Why China's Love for Putin Is Dangerous", *The Diplomat*, 6 August 2014 at https://thediplomat.com/2014/08/why-chinas-love-for-putin-is-dangerous/
36. William Yang, "Ukraine war: How Russian propaganda dominates Chinese social media", *DW*, April 6, 2022 at https://www.dw.com/en/ukraine-war-how-russian-propaganda-dominates-chinese-social-media/a-61375386
37. Zhu Ying, "Weibo a new 'battlefield' of words in Russia-Ukraine crisis", *Shine*, 24 February 2022 at https://www.shine.cn/opinion/2202242305/
38. Ashley Gold, "China's state media buys Meta ads pushing Russia's line on war", *Axios*, 9 March 2022 at https://www.axios.com/2022/03/09/chinas-state-media-meta-facebook-ads-russia
39. Institut Montaigne, "The China-Ukraine Partnership: Surviving a Deteriorating Strategic Environment", 9 February 2022 at https://www.institutmontaigne.org/en/blog/china-ukraine-partnership-surviving-deteriorating-strategic-environment
40. Ibid.

41. Natasha Kuhrt and Marcin Kaczmarski, "Ukraine invasion: why China is more likely to support Russia than in the past", *The Conversation*, 22 February 2022, https://theconversation.com/ukraine-invasion-why-china-is-more-likely-to-support-russia-than-in-the-past-177854
42. Ukrinform, "China will never attack Ukraine, ambassador assures", at https://www.ukrinform.net/rubric-polytics/3430195-china-will-never-attack-ukraine-ambassador-assures.html
43. Liu Zhen, "China sends first shipment of humanitarian aid to Ukraine", *South China Morning Post*, 9 March 2022 at https://www.scmp.com/news/china/diplomacy/article/3169853/china-sends-first-shipment-humanitarian-aid-ukraine
44. Reuters, "China offers additional $1.57 million humanitarian aid to Ukraine", *India Today*, 21 March 2022 at https://www.indiatoday.in/world/russia-ukraine-war/story/china-1-57-million-humanitarian-aid-ukraine-1927775-2022-03-21
45. Chao Deng, "China Offers 'Necessary Mediation', Aid to Ukraine", *The Wall Street Journal*, 7 March 2022 at https://www.wsj.com/livecoverage/russia-ukraine-latest-news-2022-03-07/card/china-offers-necessary-mediation-aid-to-ukraine-auaEVkbq198QD1Xc6aTV
46. Ukrinform, "China will never attack Ukraine, ambassador assures", at https://www.ukrinform.net/rubric-polytics/3430195-china-will-never-attack-ukraine-ambassador-assures.html
47. Yongnian Zheng in Wang Gungwu and John Wong (eds.), *Comprehensive National Power: An Expression of China's New Nationalism* (1998) London: World Scientific.
48. Xi Jinping, "Secure a Decisive Victory in Building a Moderately Prosperous Society in All Respects and Strive for the Great Success of Socialism with Chinese Characteristics for a New Era", speech delivered at the 19th National Congress of the Communist Party of China, October 18, 2017, at https://www.mfa.gov.cn/ce/ceil/eng/zt/19thCPCNationalCongress/W020171120127269060039.pdf
49. Nathan Hutson, "War in Ukraine is hamstringing China's 'Belt and Road Initiative'", *Responsible Statecraft*, 22 March 2022, at https://responsiblestatecraft.org/2022/03/22/beltandroadchinarussia/

CHAPTER 2

Can China Emulate Russian Aggression in Taiwan?

Manoj Kumar Panigrahi

ABSTRACT

Since the first shot of Russia's military adventure into Ukraine began on 24 February 2022, there have been multiple comparisons with other disputes worldwide. One such comparison done is between the China-Taiwan relations which is also known as Cross-strait relations. It is anticipated by some that the Chinese will do a quick and short invasion and shall be able to control Taiwan and its other islands. Chinese leaders have always tested waters in the strait to gauge the responses of the Taiwanese and its security guarantor the United States by increasing the military flights or using coastguard and other means. With the conflict between Ukraine-Russian sides having dragged over the earlier anticipated time, the Taiwanese and its well-wishers have some assurances that the Chinese leaders have now to re-think their plan of capturing the island by force. This chapter will explore the Cross-strait relations based on Taiwan as a small power trying to balance and bandwagon its relationship with the US and China. The question to be explored is- Will the Chinese be able to use the military option in taking over its claim in Taiwan? By using the concept of "Push and Pull" this chapter argues that the Chinese leaders have more to lose if they try to use force than the Russians lost during their invasion of Ukraine.

Key words: *Russia-Ukraine, China-Taiwan, Military relations, small power, Identity vs. Interest.*

Introduction

On the morning of 20 April 2022, at 7.11 am (local time), Taiwan[1] woke up to an unusual news item on television. Screens showed the title *'New Taipei City hit by Chinese missile, Port of Taipei warship explodes, facilities, vessels damaged, President issues emergency decree'*.[2]

Such news flashes appeared on the channel run by the Chinese Television System (CTS), based out of Taiwan, though, to the luck of the local Taiwanese and others, the doomsday titles were a mistake. Later, the CTS issued a public apology stating that the texts were from disaster drill messages and had been aired mistakenly.[3] CTS removed the report later, but it still brought the ire of the security agencies on the forum. Such news (even though a mistake) created panic on the social media platforms in Taiwan.

Since the first shot of Russia's military adventure into Ukraine was fired on 24 February 2022,[4] there have been multiple comparisons with other disputes worldwide. One such comparison is between China-Taiwan relations, also known as 'Cross-Strait relations'. Some anticipate that the Chinese will do a quick and short invasion and will be able to control mainland Taiwan and its other outlying islands, which are closer to China than Taiwan itself. Chinese leaders have constantly tested waters in the Strait to gauge the responses of the Taiwanese and its security guarantor, the USA, by increasing military flights or using the coast guard and other means. The conflict between Ukraine and Russia having dragged over the earlier anticipated time, the Taiwanese and their well-wishers have some assurance that the Chinese leaders must now re-think their plan to capture the island by force.

This chapter explores the cross-Strait relations based on Taiwan as a small power trying to balance and bandwagon its relationship between the USA and China. The question analysed is: Will the Chinese be able to use the military option to take over its claim in Taiwan? This chapter argues that the Chinese leaders have more to lose than gain if they try to use force against Taiwan at this current stage.

The chapter, at the outset, discusses the background of the cross-Strait relations by identifying key events when the People's Republic of China (PRC)[5] tried to take over Taiwan militarily. The framework of *'push and pull'* describes the existing cross-Strait relations. The chapter also explores several attempts by the PRC to test the response patterns of the Republic of China (ROC) and the USA since Xi Jinping came to power in 2012. This chapter also highlights several challenges to Taiwan's responses toward China. It then explains how the Taiwanese government has attempted to address these sticky issues. The chapter fleshes out several independent variables to show that China's military response to the Taiwan issue will be short-sighted.

Background

In order to understand from where the current fears of invasion of Taiwan emerge, a cursory look at history becomes essential. After Japan's surrender upon its defeat in World War II in 1945, Taiwan was transferred to the Chiang Kai-shek-led ROC government (there was no official control over Taiwan during that period by China) based in Mainland China. Chiang Kai-shek ruled the island robustly and in a heavy-handed manner through his generals. It led to multiple incidents, such as 228, where on 28 February 1947, a cigarette seller was brutally beaten and killed, which led to a massive island-wide protest against the Kuomintang (KMT).[6] The uprising led to a massive crackdown by the KMT/ROC forces. It was followed by years of martial law, termed 'White Terror'.[7] The number of people executed in this period ranges between 10,000 and 30,000.[8]

Following his defeat at the hands of the Mao Zedong-led communist forces in 1949, Chiang Kai-shek moved to Taiwan with KMT nationalist soldiers and his followers. The KMT leader believed he would be able to return to the 'motherland' one day. On the other hand, Mao Zedong led the Chinese Communist Party (CCP), and the successive leaders of China to see Taiwan as 'unfinished business.[9] They have to make it free and liberate Taiwan and its residents. It was not until 14 July 1987 that Martial Law was lifted in Taiwan after the sacrifice of many individuals who were tortured, jailed, and killed for raising their voice against the dictatorship.

External factors played a crucial role in developing cross-Strait relations, such as the Korean War (1950-1953), the Cold War between the USA and Soviet Russia that was brewing, and Chiang Kai-shek's attempt to stabilise his position over Taiwan and the USA government to sign the 1954 US-ROC Mutual Defence Treaty.[10]

The treaty came under a tough test multiple times between 1954 and 1958 when the Mao Zedong-led People's Liberation Army (PLA) attempted to take over the offshore islands of Kinmen and Mazu, which were under KMT control.[11] However, the military takeover of the offshore islands did not meet its objective, causing a long pause on military action against Taiwan besides bombing the islands with an artillery barrage on alternate days until 15 December 1979.

Post-1978, the next big crisis in cross-Strait relations was in 1995-1996. The Chinese government fired missiles into the Taiwan Strait to respond to the speech of the then-President of Taiwan, Lee Teng-hui (1988-2000) at Cornell University.[12,13] Beijing claimed it was pushing away from the idea of the 'One China' policy as agreed to between China and Taiwan earlier. Again, the missile crisis tested the USA-ROC (Taiwan) treaty. It led USA aircraft carriers to sail into the Taiwan Strait, sending a message that the USA would intervene if the situation escalated into a full-blown military operation.[14]

'Push and Pull' in the Cross-Strait Relations

The idea of 'push and pull factors' is relevant to studying cross-Strait relations. To define, 'push' is that action that lets a country, organisation, or individual make decisions. Such actions are a result of either internal or external factors or both. It can lead to either a desired or an undesired result for the actors through which the push is initiated. It usually results in a chain reaction of 'push' actions if a third party is involved.

N. Harris, in his work about untouchable immigrants, has explained the 'push and pull'. As per Harris, the determinants that cause an entity, state, or people to go out of their way are called 'push factors', while those that attract them to a particular destination are called 'pull factors'.[15]

'Pull' is that action that leads a country to change the status quo of a situation. It can also be influenced by internal and external actors with varying degrees of the desired result. Both 'push and pull' challenge the *agreed-upon status quo* by two or more parties.

In the context of the Ukraine-Russia conflict and its reflections on Northeast Asia, the concept of 'push and pull' becomes pertinent, along with the usage of two different empirical cases.

For instance, the USA and its allies influenced and 'pushed' Ukraine to lean more towards the West.. Such actions resulted in Russian President Vladimir Putin launching a military offensive against Ukraine.[16] The 'push' from the USA and its allies was followed by public statements by Ukrainian leaders to join the European Union and the North Atlantic Treaty Organisation (NATO).[17] Against this backdrop, President Putin's action of launching the war can be explained as the result of the 'pull' action done by Ukraine against the status quo of the regional order, which was agreed upon earlier.

In his statement, Ukrainian Presidential spokesman Sergii Nykyforov mentioned that joining NATO and the European Union is an *'absolute priority.*[18] Such 'push' initiated the military approach by the Russian side, who saw the move to join NATO by Ukraine as a larger encirclement by the USA and its allies. Millions have been displaced, and multiple attempts to stop the fight have been unsuccessful. Since the war has raged on, there have been concessions from the Ukrainian side when it gave up its attempt to join NATO. Ukrainian President Volodymyr Zelenskyy, in his statement, stated, *'I cooled down regarding this question a long time ago after we understood that...NATO is not prepared to accept Ukraine'*.[19]

On similar grounds, while bringing the concept of 'push and pull' to cross-Strait relations, multiple associated factors must be considered. For ease of understanding, two independent variables are chosen—political and economic. Taiwan's unique situation of not being recognised as a country on most international platforms—only by 14 countries—is a critical criterion in this context. (Given Taiwan's unique situation of not being recognised as a country on almost all international platforms and officially only recognised as a country by 14 countries[20], it has become one of the critical criteria). On the economic front, Taiwan significantly depends on China for most of its trade (elaborated in a later section).

The current situation maintains the status quo of Taiwan not declaring independence and China not declaring a military offensive against Taiwan. Furthermore, on the economic front, Taiwanese companies are operating in large numbers in China, which has led to interdependence. Taiwanese companies in China enjoy a similar cultural and language environment and geographical proximity. At the same time, the Chinese side has enjoyed a high growth rate due to such investments and has been able to use economic interdependence to attract talent from Taiwan. In order to answer the central question of whether China will emulate a

Russian-style attack in Taiwan, it becomes pertinent to imagine the scenarios wherein key players influence the decision for China to unleash aggression on Taiwan.

Figure 2.1 depicts the push-and pull between Taiwan and China and how external actors influence both sides of the Strait. For the cross-Strait relationship, the USA has been taken as an external actor that determines the region's external influence and has leverage on both sides of the Straits regarding peace or conflict between Taiwan and China.

Figure 2.1: Conceptual Framework on Cross-Strait Peace and War

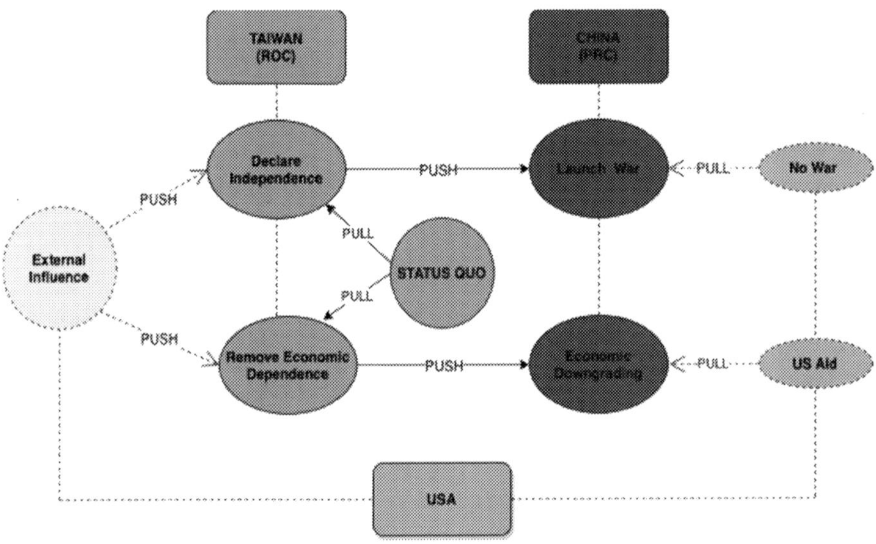

In situation one (S1), where the USA becomes an external actor, if it 'pushes' Taiwan, or Taiwan itself, due to its domestic factors 'pulls' itself from the status quo for declaring independence, it 'pushes' China to launch a war against Taiwan. Nevertheless, as per the 1954 Mutual Defence Treaty between the ROC and the USA, the latter has interfered and might interfere again, 'pulling' China against launching a war.

In situation two (S2), the USA tries to 'push' Taiwan to remove its economic dependence on China. Alternatively, when Taiwan tries to 'pull' itself away by removing its economic dependence on China, it will drastically affect the Taiwanese economy and lose its competitive edge. Suppose Taiwanese companies find an alternative to the Chinese production line. In that case, it will be another challenge to the business community of Taiwan because now they have to deal with an unchartered area. A new place with new laws, different culture, and language will pose quite a challenge to businesses. In this scenario, the USA will interfere as it did in the early 1970s and 1980s, where it will give economic aid to Taiwan to stabilise its economy.

This chapter covers two incidents and issues in the following sections, each from the political, economic, and military cross-Strait relations.

Xi Jinping's Moves towards Taiwan

To understand Xi Jinping's aims of reunifying Taiwan with the mainland, it becomes pertinent to study what Chinese moves have been able to achieve or not achieve in Taiwan over the years.

In his earlier statements, China's President Xi Jinping mentioned, 'the complete reunification of our motherland is an aspiration shared by people on both sides of the Taiwan Strait'.[21] Xi Jinping also warned the USA that the Taiwan issue must be 'handled properly' to avoid harming relations between the two countries.[22]

The answer to the main question raised in this chapter of whether China can emulate Russia's Ukraine aggression on Taiwan is 'no'. China's previous military options were attempted over the offshore islands based on the earlier background discussed. The idea of a 'military takeover' of Taiwan has changed from 'hard power' to 'smart power'. Innovative power can be defined as one party using multiple ways, including hard and soft means, to change the behaviour or status quo of its targeted adversary.

Hard power can be defined as using traditional military hardware and techniques to get the desired result. In contrast, Soft Power can be termed as using non-military techniques and influencing the target to do things one wants without telling them what to do. Furthermore, Smart Power is a mix of hard and soft simultaneously to achieve the objective.

With time, China has changed its tactics to using 'smart power' instead of using only 'hard power'. The use of 'smart power' is evident in the political, economic, militarily, and a relatively new form of influence operations known as cognitive warfare.

Since Xi Jinping came to power in China in 2013, Taiwan has seen a significant number of countries that de-recognised it as an independent. In 2013, Taiwan was recognised as a nation by 23 countries, falling to 14 as in May 2022.[23] There is speculation that there may be more countries to follow those who might de-recognise Taiwan as a country.

The promise of 'political and economic gain' has led multiple countries to switch sides in cross-Strait relations. One of the reasons that can be articulated for such a behaviour change is that China has more to offer than Taiwan. Providing a larger market for the goods produced, infrastructure loans, and other support needed for its citizens, such as student scholarships, has led the countries to switch ties from Taiwan to China. Such a switch for economic reasons has been termed 'cheque-book diplomacy'.[24]

On the anniversary of the revolution that overthrew the Qing Imperial dynasty in China in 1911, Xi Jinping 2021 mentioned that 'Taiwan independence separatism is the biggest obstacle to achieving the reunification of the motherland and the most serious hidden danger to national rejuvenation.'[25] Through such statements, it is quite pertinent that China is not ready to give up its claim over Taiwan and hopes that Taiwan will be unified to 'Greater China' one day.

Another political move made by the Chinese to undermine Taiwan has been the issuance of the 'Mainland Compatriot Permit', also known as the 'Taiwan Compatriot Permit'. China's Ministry of Public Security issues a permit for Taiwanese nationals with household registration in Taiwan to enter mainland China. This permit allows Taiwanese to travel to and from China and is considered and widely used as an identity document for Taiwanese in China.[26]

As the Taiwanese passport is not recognised in China, such a permit is issued to make Taiwanese nationals a part of China. By availing such a permit, Taiwanese can now access China's basic old-age insurance plan. Additionally, if they choose to leave China before meeting the requirements, they can choose to do so. Besides a national policy, municipalities and provinces of China offer multiple benefits to attract Taiwanese. As per the *Qiushi*, a CCP Central Committee bimonthly report, Zhu Fenglian, spokesperson for the Taiwan Affairs Office of the State Council, said that the 'mainland will continue to implement policies treating Taiwan compatriots as equals with more concrete actions to address their problems'.[27]

Using the words 'compatriots' instead of 'nationals' reflects multiple fronts. First, the Taiwanese are not seen as separate nationals per se; they are treated to be more inclusive. Second, such an inclusive policy lets the Taiwanese have a favourable attitude towards Beijing, where they are treated on the same terms on social schemes, insurance, and other eighteen schemes and policies.[28] Giving the Taiwanese such perks reflects Beijing's ambition to influence the 'hearts and minds' of the Taiwanese, which might put pressure on the government in Taiwan to have a more favourable attitude towards China.

In terms of economic coercion, there have been multiple steps from China involving Taiwan. In the 1980s, when China opened its economy to the world, Taiwanese enterprises took one of the first steps to invest and move their production lines to China.[29] The Taiwanese business community in China is popularly known as *Taishang*. From 1986 to 1991, between 2,500 and 4,000 Taiwanese companies invested approximately 3 billion USD in China. By June 1993, it reached 14.5 billion USD.[30]

Nevertheless, the investments have sharply declined since President Xi Jinping took the leadership role in China. It is pretty evident as per the data available at Statista from 2011 until 2021. Table 2.1 depicts the value of approved Foreign Direct Investments (FDI) from Taiwan to Mainland China.

Table 2.1: Value of approved Foreign Direct Investments (FDI) from Taiwan into Mainland China

	2011	*2012*	*2013*	*2014*	*2015*	*2016*	*2017*	*2018*	*2019*	*2020*	*2021*
Amount (in billion USD)	14.38	12.79	9.19	10.28	10.97	9.67	9.25	8.5	4.17	5.91	5.86

Source: Statista[31]

Since 2013, the approved FDI from Taiwan to China has sharply declined from 9.19 billion USD to 5.86 billion USD in 2021. The decline of the FDI has multiple explanations. First, there has been a declining trend among the Taiwanese leadership to let investments be approved towards China. Secondly, it can also be interpreted that the Chinese leadership has toughened its stand and is selective on what investments it can receive from the Taiwanese..

Beijing has also increasingly targeted those Taiwanese companies that have either donated to or supported the elections campaigns in Taiwan.

Zhu Fenglian, in his statement, mentioned that 'We (China) will not allow any company to make money in the Chinese mainland and then donate money to diehard Taiwanese independence groups'.[32]

In 2021, China imposed a fine of 13.87 million USD on Taiwan's Far Eastern Group's mainland subsidiary for violations, including breaches of environmental protection rules.[33] Such a fine was a surprise to many because the company has close ties with the leadership on both sides of the Straits, and it was giving an equal amount of donations to the independence-leaning Democratic Progressive Party (DPP) and the KMT, which is considered China-friendly.[34]

Labour costs are rising in China, and most Taiwanese companies that have invested there have seen a sharp decline in revenue over time. Such a decline in revenue is evident when comparing the data of investments made by Taiwanese companies and the number of remittances sent back to Taiwan. Since 2013, the remittances sent to Taiwan have declined from 4.2 billion USD to 578 million USD in June 2020.[35] Such a significant decline reflects that the investment environment and the USA-China trade war have affected the *Taishang* community looking for investments in China.

It becomes pertinent to analyse the multiple predictions around the cross-Strait relations, which have existed since 1949. As discussed earlier, past attempts by China to take control over the geographically closer Matsu and Kinmen islands failed. The second attempt, the 1995-1996 missile crisis, saw the USA sailing its naval ships across the Taiwan Strait.

If one compares the military capabilities of both sides, there is a significant difference in terms of budget, active service members, military hardware, and one's self-sustaining defence industry. China has a greater economy, a large population and resources, and the military's upper hand. As per Global Firepower, which ranks countries based on their military and financial strengths, China ranks three and Taiwan 21 out of 142 countries.[36]

An Air Defence Identification Zone (ADIZ) exists between nations worldwide. It serves as a buffer between international airspace and a country's territorial airspace, extending 12 nautical miles from a country's coast.[37] The so-called ADIZ also exists between China and Taiwan. Both sides follow an imaginary line drawn by the USA in 1955, delineating both sides of the Strait.[38]

One aspect of China's military used against Taiwan is its airpower. Since 2016, when Tsai-ing Wen's DPP party, which is pro-independence, took over the leadership role of Taiwan's presidentship, China's number of such military flights has taken a great leap. Air incursions across the ADIZ by the Chinese air force have increased. As per data compiled through various news reports and Ministry of Defence, Taiwan, reports, the ADIZ incursions by China from August 2016 until December 2017 stands at 26, for 2018 it was 638, for 2019 it was 675, for 2020 it stands at 380, and for 2021 it rose significantly to 969. Until 6 May, 2022, the number stands at 370.[39]

Such a rise of increased flights has been termed as a tactic by the Chinese to make the limited resources of the Taiwanese air force stretch thin and make such flights to make the Chinese air force trainee pilots get used to some actual combat situations and check the response of the Taiwanese military.

Another military aspect closely followed by the Chinese is the support from the USA to Taiwan to maintain the defence preparedness of the Taiwanese. Taiwan's military hardware primarily consists of the USA's, which it can purchase through the Taiwan Relations Act of 1979.[40] On 18 November 2021, President Tsai Ing-wen commissioned 64 advanced F-16V 'Viper' fighter jets into service. Such an upgraded version of fighter jets was inducted to maintain the aerial combat balance.[41] The upgraded jets will form the core of the Taiwanese air defence to ward off any attack. It is not a hidden fact that the Taiwanese air force lacks numbers to go on an air duel if China decides to launch a full-scale military attack.

Different administrations of the USA have had different policies on how much arms the USA can send to Taiwan. Each time such arms sales are done, the Chinese government follows with a strong statement, ADIZ incursions and sailing its aircraft carrier group around Taiwan. The US Administration 2022 decided to sell the Patriot Air Defence system to Taiwan. In response to the sale on 8 February 2022, China's Foreign Ministry spokesperson Zhao Lijian, in a press briefing, asked for 'immediately revoking' and added, 'China will take legitimate and strong measures to defend its sovereignty and security interests. As for the specific measures, please wait and see'.[42]

China's 'push and pull' towards the Straits have been unique to its behaviour with changing leadership. Under Xi Jinping, the aggressiveness has only increased towards Taiwan and other countries with which China has disputes. It has land boundary issues with India, Bhutan and disputed claims over the South China Sea. Studying the Taiwanese responses to Chinese aggression in this context becomes pertinent.

Taiwan's Response to Xi Jinping's Strategy

In 2016, President Tsai mentioned that her administration would take a fresh look at cross-Strait relations in her first inaugural speech. She talked about how the cross-Strait relations will advance under the ROC Constitution, and both sides (Taiwan and China) must set aside the baggage of history, and engage in positive dialogue, for the benefit of the people on both sides.[43]

Making the ROC Constitution a base for engagement in cross-Strait relations changed how Taiwan and China conducted talks to sort out the differences. Such a move by Tsai Ing-wen was seen as a step closer to independence by Beijing, and it became one of the reasons that caused a significant loss of diplomatic allies to Taiwan.

Taiwan follows a democratic system, where public opinion matters in shaping its foreign policy. A poll conducted by the Taiwan Public Opinion Foundation (TPOF) in December 2021 found that about 60.1 per cent of those polled said they did not care about Taiwan losing allies. Only 32.5 per cent of those polled said they were worried about the issue. Such a wide gap in foreign allies reflects the lack of awareness among the local Taiwanese.[44]

Former Taiwanese Foreign Minister Chen Chien-Jen, in 2016, stated that 'even if Taiwan ended up with no diplomatic allies in its present form as the ROC, it could gain allies as an independent Taiwan'.[45] Such a change of attitude reflects a strategic shift among the Taiwanese public and diplomats that having diplomatic allies is not something they are vouching for as long as it does not change the region's status quo. As per one of the analysts, Lev Nachman, the Taiwanese strategy is to develop informal relations with like-minded nations based on democracy and values.[46] Therefore, losing such allies when most of the domestic audience does not know where such allies are located seemed insignificant.

Traditionally, the USA has been the significant security guarantor of Taiwan. For its survivability and primary arms supply, it has maintained its staunch support for Taiwan. The USA's primary goal in the region is to avoid changing the status quo. Instead, it is political, military, and economical. Moreover, it hopes that the cross-Strait relations are solved quickly and peacefully. It has opposed any changes to the status quo attempted by both sides of the Straits.

Tsai Ing-wen's presidentship and her party, the DPP, took power in 2016 from the President Ma Ying-jeou-led KMT party. Although the power transition was smooth, multiple issues rocked President Ma's rule. One of the critical issues was the 2013 Cross-Strait Service Trade Agreement (CSSTA) trade pact signed with China, which opened up the economy and selected industries for investments. The CSSTA was a follow-up agreement to the Economic Cooperation Framework Agreement (ECFA) signed in 2010, similar to Free Trade agreements signed between other nations in the world. Such an agreement was seen as surrendering Taiwan's sovereignty and sacrificing the domestic market. It led to a massive protest by youth leaders and saw comprehensive support from the DPP and other political parties, popularly known as the 'Sunflower Movement'.[47] Such movements show an active interest in domestic politics among the youth of Taiwan, and they are wary of changes happening inside Taiwan concerning cross-Strait relations.

Taiwan's response to the political moves made by the Chinese has been multi-fold. It has been straightforward in winning a number of diplomatic allies. In 2019, when Kiribati denounced its relationship with Taiwan, President Tsai said such a move was a 'regrettable decision' and accused China of influencing Taiwan's 2020 Presidential election, in which President Tsai was running for her second term. President Tsai also highlighted the Chinese use of 'money and political pressure' to undermine Taiwanese diplomatic allies. In December 2021, Taiwan lost its ally, Nicaragua, to China. In her statement, President Tsai talked about the values of democracy, 'The more successful Taiwan's democracy, and the greater the international support, the greater the pressure from the authoritarian camp'.[48]

Such statements by the Taiwanese leadership reflect the importance it puts on democracy and shared common values rather than coercion and, as mentioned earlier, 'cheque-book diplomacy'. There has been staunch support from the USA against any change to the status quo of the cross-Strait relationship.

The response to the Chinese inclusion of Mainland Compatriots was lacklustre from the Taiwanese except those looking to work in China or had some business interests in the mainland. As per the author's personal experience, such news was downplayed by multiple media channels and the Taiwanese people.

Under the current geopolitical setting, including the USA-China trade war that began with the Trump Administration, China's *Taishang* community was affected the most. Like most Taiwanese companies that set up their manufacturing base in China to export to the USA, such sanctions against China-manufactured goods affected the production and business of such industries.

President Tsai Ing-wen and her administration re-launched the New Southbound Policy (NSP) soon after taking over the presidentship in May 2016. The NSP aims to increase ties in several sectors[49] with South Asia, South East Asia, Australia and New Zealand. This led to continuous targeted fines and warnings from the Chinese side to the *Taishang* community and fining the conglomerates that have donated or spoken in favour of an independent Taiwan. Since the launch of the NSP policy, there has been a significant increase in trade and investment between Taiwan and NSP countries.

In 2016, Taiwan's investment flowed to South-East Asian countries, reaching 4.2 billion USD, whereas in 2017, investments in Singapore, Indonesia, Malaysia, the Philippines, Thailand, and Vietnam reached 2.82 billion USD. While investments in India in 2017 reached 30.56 million USD, in Australia they stood at 615.88 million USD.[50]

As of 2021, Taiwanese investments in the first 11 months saw Southeast Asia sharing 37 per cent compared to 33 per cent for China.[51] Such a meteoric rise in investments into NSP countries can be seen as staunch support from the Taiwanese officials to unlock themselves from the overdependence on China for their growth.

The trade war has also pushed some Taiwanese companies to return to Taiwan's home turf. Such companies were provided with preferential treatment in terms of tax and other facilities in specific economic zones. As per the latest data available in 2019, the inbound investments done by Taiwanese companies returning from China stood at 1.29 billion USD creating 4,400 jobs in Taiwan.[52] It is also speculated that such a rise in investments has increased the Taiwanese's largely stagnated monthly salary.

Another aspect of economic reboots is, amid challenges from China, that Taiwan has adopted is its attempt to join international trade blocs. Taiwan showed enthusiasm for joining the trans-Pacific trade bloc, bilateral free-trade agreement (Taiwan signed such ones with Singapore and New Zealand in 2013) and attempting a few more trade talks bilaterally with the USA and possibly with India. Such attempts were made to improve the competitiveness of Taiwanese products and to increase their visibility. India is considered an alternative to the Taiwanese business manufacturing units in China. If such an agreement is signed, it will significantly boost both sides. India will get much-needed investments for its 'Make in India' policy by providing jobs and economic growth. Moreover, Taiwan will be assured of a steady supply of talent at a low cost and keep its strategic advantage over globally semiconductor and electronics products.

Given Taiwan's stronghold over semiconductors globally, it is also anticipated that it has provided a *semiconductor shield* to Taiwan regarding any military offensive by China. With the global supply chain already constrained due to the COVID-19 pandemic, there is a wide existential gap between the world's demand and supply of semiconductors. An armed conflict between China and Taiwan will create ripple effects worldwide.

Regarding the military preparedness of Taiwan, the major challenge it faces is being outnumbered in terms of military hardware compared to China. Most of Taiwan's weapons are defensive. If a conflict occurs between the two sides of the Straits, soldiers from China will attempt an aerial drop over key strategic bases and buildings of Taiwan or in the offshore islands, which are geographically closer to Taiwan.

However, it is also true that both Chinese and Taiwanese soldiers have not experienced active combat for decades, and active Taiwanese soldiers are numerically much less than the Chinese. A few analysts also described Taiwan as a 'porcupine' if there is a war. The idea is to show how much damage Taiwan can inflict on an adversary so that China does not even attempt risk invading it.[53]

Multiple domestic challenges to the Taiwanese military pose a tough nut to crack on its defence preparedness against China. Firstly, the youth consider it a 'waste of time' to join the military. Such a defensive approach also comes at a risk when most youth think joining the military is not something they look forward to. Military conscription of four months for those born after 1993 is considered a significant issue. Secondly, many conscripts dodge training. About 1,000 reservists were charged between 2014 and 2017 for not attending their training.[54]

If there is no such push for the people to join the army and its dwindling population, the 'porcupine' that everyone expects Taiwan to be would lack its pointedness against the Chinese invasion.

Conclusion

Whether China can emulate the Russian invasion of Ukraine in Taiwan is not easy to answer, as there are multiple factors to consider. Each side has its strength and weakness. Taiwan has the assurance of the USA's support if China attempts to change the status quo militarily. The US armed forces have conducted regular Freedom of Navigation (FON) exercises in the Taiwan Straits in the past and in the present.

As mentioned earlier, the Chinese have started using 'smart power' rather than relying only on 'hard power' or 'economic coercion'. There has been a significant rise in influencing operations and interfering in Taiwan's domestic politics and with daily life regarding fake news about COVID-19 vaccination among Taiwanese social media platforms, Professional Technology Temple (PTT) and D-Card.

However, an unexpected fallout of the Chinese usage of smart power is that the Taiwanese identity has also strengthened over the years. The growing sense of a separate Taiwanese identity is quite evident from the survey conducted by the Election Study Centre, National Chengchi University. Table 2.2 depicts how the people who live in Taiwan identify themselves.

Table 2.2: Chinese/Taiwanese Identity of Taiwanese (in %)

Year	*Taiwanese*	*Both Taiwanese and Chinese*	*Chinese*	*No Response*
1992	17.6	46.4	25.5	10.5
2012	54.3	38.5	3.6	3.6
2021	62.3	31.7	2.8	3.2

Source: Election Study Centre, National Chengchi University.[55]

As per Table 2.2, the survey conducted in Taiwan shows that since it was taken first in 1992, the sense of individual Taiwanese identity, different from that of the PRC, has increased from only 17.6 per cent in 1992 to 62.3 per cent in 2021. At the same time, those who identify themselves as both Taiwanese and Chinese have reduced from 46.4 per cent in 1992 to 31.7 per cent in 2021. In contrast, the percentage of people identifying themselves as only Chinese has drastically changed from 25.5 per cent in 1992 to 2.8 per cent in 2021. The reduction in the Chinese identity implies a change of 'identity' among the people staying in Taiwan. Such strong self-identification of self as 'Taiwanese' has been on an upward trend since 1992 when the survey was conducted.

The 'push and pull' between the two sides politically needs to find its balance which, if not maintained properly, might lead to an armed conflict leading to further percussions between China, the USA, and its allies in the region.

ENDNOTES

1. The official name of Taiwan is Republic of China (ROC). To maintain consistency, Taiwan will be used throughout the chapter.
2. S. Chiang "Taiwanese news station mistakenly broadcasts 'breaking news' of Chinese invasion", *Taiwan News* 20 April 2022: https://www.taiwannews.com.tw/en/news/4513019
3. 'CTS *華視道歉聲明 (CTS Apology Statement)'. CTS,* 20 April 2022: https://www.cts.com.tw/notify.php
4. J. Psaropoulos, 'Timeline: A month of Russia's war in Ukraine'. *Al Jazeera,* 23 March 2022: https://www.aljazeera.com/news/2022/3/23/timeline-a-month-of-war-in-ukraine
5. The official name of China is People's Republic of China (PRC). To maintain consistency, China will be used throughout the chapter.
6. To maintain consistency, Kuomintang (KMT) and Republic of China (ROC) will be used simultaneously.
7. Wang, P. C.-m, A Bastion Created, a Regime Reformed, an Economy Reengineered, 1949-1970. in M.A. Rubinstein, *Taiwan A New History,* New York: Routledge, 2015
8. J. Chung, 'White Terror database released', *Taipei Times* 27 February 2020: https://www.taipeitimes.com/News/taiwan/archives/2020/02/27/2003731700
9. L. Hornby 'China: Why Taiwan is unfinished business for Xi Jinping'. *Financial Times* 22 September 2019: https://www.ft.com/content/357f8ab8-d088-11e9-99a4-b5ded7a7fe3f?list=intlhomepage
10. D. Huang A.-c. *'The United States and Taiwan's Defense Transformation'.* Brookings 16 February 2010: https://www.brookings.edu/opinions/the-united-states-and-taiwans-defense-transformation/
11. D. Fell, *Government and Politics in Taiwan.* Oxon: Routledge, 2012, p. 16.

12. Full speech can be accessed at: https://www.president.gov.tw/NEWS/22622
13. S. Lijun, *'China's Dilemma-The Taiwan Issue'*. Singapore: I.B. Tauris & Co. Ltd., 2001, p. 157.
14. D. Priest & J. Havemann, 'Second Group of U.S. Ships sent to Taiwan'. *The Washington Post,* 11 March 1996: https://www.washingtonpost.com/archive/politics/1996/03/11/second-group-of-us-ships-sent-to-taiwan/34280337-be79-4d6e-b859-8046682a37b3/
15. N. Harris, *'The new untouchables-Immigrant and the New World Workers'*. New York: Penguin, 1995.
16. J. J. Mearsheimer, *'Why the Ukraine Crisis Is the West's Fault: The Liberal Delusions That Provoked Putin'*. 2014, September/October, *Foreign Affairs,* 93(5), 85-89.
17. D.W., 'Ukraine reaffirms desire to join NATO after envoy comments'. *DW Made for minds* 14 February 2022: https://www.dw.com/en/ukraine-reaffirms-desire-to-join-nato-after-envoy-comments/a-60768298
18. Ibid.
19. France24, 'In nod to Russia, Ukraine says no longer insisting on NATO membership'. *France24,* 8 March 2022 : https://www.france24.com/en/live-news/20220308-in-nod-to-russia-ukraine-says-no-longer-insisting-on-nato-membership
20. The countries are: Marshall Islands, Republic of Nauru, Palau, Tuvalu, Eswatini, Holy See, Belize, Republic of Guatemala, Haiti, Republic of Honduras, Paraguay, Federation of Saint Christopher and Nevis, St. Lucia, and Saint Vincent and the Grenadines (as of May 22, 2022) [(MOFA (Taiwan-ROC), 2022)].
21. 'Xi Jinping flags Taiwan reunification, CPC achievements in his New Year address'. *The Economic Times,* 31 December 2021: https://economictimes.indiatimes.com/news/international/world-news/xi-jinping-flags-taiwan-reunification-cpc-achievements-in-his-new-year-address/articleshow/88619664.cms
22. "Xi tells US to handle Taiwan 'properly' to avoid damaging ties". *Al Jazeera* 19 March 2022: https://www.aljazeera.com/news/2022/3/19/xi-warns-us-over-taiwan-impact-on-relations
23. 'Diplomatic Allies', *Ministry of Foreign Affairs, Republic of China (Taiwan)* 22 May 2022, https://en.mofa.gov.tw/AlliesIndex.aspx?n=1294&sms=1007#Accesskey_U
24. 'China's cheque-book diplomacy.', *Deccan Chronicle* 17 April 2017: https://www.deccanchronicle.com/opinion/op-ed/170417/chinas-cheque-book-diplomacy.html
25. C. Garcia, & Y.L. Tian, 'China's Xi vows 'reunification' with Taiwan'. 10 October 2021 *Reuters*: https://www.reuters.com/world/china/chinas-xi-says-reunification-with-taiwan-must-will-be-realised-2021-10-09/
26. Thomson, 'Taiwan compatriot permit (台湾居民来往大陆通行证)'. *Thomson Reuters Practical Law* 2022: https://uk.practicallaw.thomsonreuters.com/5-586-8168?transition Type=Default&contextData=(sc.Default)&firstPage=true
27. Qiushi, 'Mainland opens door wider for Taiwan compatriots'. CPC Central Committee Bimonthly *Qiushi,* 29 July 2021: http://en.qstheory.cn/2021-07/29/c_647020.htm
28. SCMP, 'New ID card to give Hong Kong, Macau and Taiwan residents access to public services on mainland China'. *South China Morning Post* 16 August 2018: https://www.scmp.com/video/china/2160040/new-id-card-give-hong-kong-macau-and-taiwan-residents-access-public-services
29. X. Chen, "Taiwan Investments in China and Southeast Asia: 'Go West, but Also

Go South'". *Asian Survey,* 36(5), May 1996 p. 447.
30. Ibid., p. 451.
31. C. Textor. 'Value of Approved FDI from Taiwan to Mainland China from 2011 to 2021'. *Statista,* 1 March 2022: https://www.statista.com/statistics/1292815/taiwan-approved-foreign-direct-investment-into-mainland-china/
32. E. Olcott & E. Hale, 'Beijing targets Taiwanese companies with operations in China'. *Financial Times* 29 November 2021: https://www.ft.com/content/4a8515ae-69a0-4230-b7ca-329ebacd3936
33. L. Chung, 'Fines on Taiwan's Far Eastern Group fan fears of more retaliation by Beijing over political donations', *South China Morning Post,* 24 November 2021: https://www.scmp.com/news/china/politics/article/3157108/fines-taiwans-far-eastern-group-fan-fears-more-retaliation
34. E. Olcott & E. Hale, 'Beijing targets Taiwanese companies with operations in China'. *Financial Times,* 29 November 2021: https://www.ft.com/content/4a8515ae-69a0-4230-b7ca-329ebacd3936
35. K. Hille, K. (2021, 11 January). 'Taiwan manufacturers quit China over trade tensions and rising costs'. 11 January 2021, *Financial Times:* https://www.ft.com/content/5b78a04d-e51d-45d8-b276-2bbf9b11bed2
36. GFP, 'Comparison of Taiwan and China Military Strengths (2022)', *Global Fire Power* 2022: https://www.globalfirepower.com/countries-comparison-detail.php?country1=taiwan&country2=china
37. M. Trent, 'Over the Line: The Implications of China's ADIZ Intrusions in Northeast Asia'. *Federation of American Scientists* 2020. p. 9.
38. Ibid. pp. 22-23.
39. Sources: Ministry of Defence (ROC), Voice Of America, Focus Taiwan.
40. This was passed by the US Congress shortly after the USA ended its relations with Taiwan in 1979. It has provisions to sell arms to Taiwan to maintain a self-defence capability.
41. A. Dangwal, 'F-16 Viper: Taiwan Inducts The Most-Advanced F-16s Ever-Built; Can They Overpower PLAAF Jets In An Aerial-Duel?', *The EurAsian Times,* 19 November 2021: https://eurasiantimes.com/f-16-viper-can-taiwan-advanced-fighter-counter-chinese-plaaf/
42. J. Feng, "'Wait and See': China Vows Strong Response As U.S. Prepares to Arm Taiwan". *Newsweek,* 2 February 2022: https://www.newsweek.com/wait-see-china-vows-strong-response-us-prepares-arm-taiwan-missile-defense-1677148
43. President Office. 'Inaugural address of ROC 14th-term President Tsai Ing-wen', *Office of the President, Republic of China (Taiwan)* 20 May 2016: https://english.president.gov.tw/News/4893
44. TPOF, 'Public Opinion Poll – English Excerpt'. *Taiwanese Public Opinion Foundation,* Taipei, December 2021.
45. J. Yeh, 'Does Taiwan need diplomatic allies?' *Focus Taiwan,* 2 February 2022: https://focustaiwan.tw/politics/202202020001
46. L. Nachman, 'Taiwan Is Losing Allies. What Should Taipei (and D.C.) Do?' *China File,* 4 October 2019: https://www.chinafile.com/conversation/taiwan-losing-allies-what-should-taipei-and-dc-do
47. M. Turton, 'The economic legacy of Taiwan's Sunflower movement'. *Taipei Times,* 28 March 2022: https://www.taipeitimes.com/News/feat/archives/2022/03/28/2003775570

48. H. Wu, H. *'Taiwan loses diplomatic ally Nicaragua to China'*. ABC News, 10 December 2021: https://abcnews.go.com/International/wireStory/taiwan-loses-diplomatic-ally-nicaragua-china-81664006
49. The sectors are Economic and Trade cooperation, Talent exchanges, Resource sharing and Regional connectivity.
50. H. Marston & R.C. Bush, Taiwan's engagement with Southeast Asia is making progress under the New Southbound Policy. Brookings, 30 July 2018: https://www.brookings.edu/opinions/taiwans-engagement-with-southeast-asia-is-making-progress-under-the-new-southbound-policy/
51. R. Mulyanto (2022, 18 January). 'Taiwan makes new push to drum up Southeast Asia investment.' *Nikkei Asia,* 18 January 2022: https://asia.nikkei.com/Politics/International-relations/Taiwan-makes-new-push-to-drum-up-Southeast-Asia-investment
52. R. Jennings, 'Taiwan is finally luring companies back from China after more than 15 years of trying.' *South China Morning Post,* 21 March 2019: https://www.scmp.com/economy/china-economy/article/3002699/taiwan-finally-luring-companies-back-china-after-more-15
53. *Economist*. 'What is Taiwan's porcupine defence strategy?' *The Economist,* 10 May 2022: https://www.economist.com/the-economist-explains/2022/05/10/what-is-taiwans-porcupine-defence-strategy
54. Y. Lee, 'For Taiwan youth, military service is a hard sell despite China tension.' *Reuters* 29 October 2018: https://www.reuters.com/article/uk-taiwan-military-idUKKCN1N20UY
55. Election Study Centre. 'Taiwanese/Chinese Identity (1992/06-2021/12)'. Election Study Centre, National Chengchi University 10 January 2022: https://esc.nccu.edu.tw/PageDoc/Detail?fid=7800&id=6961

CHAPTER 3

Northeast Asia in the New Cyber Age

Divyanshu Jindal

ABSTRACT

The Russia-Ukraine war has given a glimpse of how the future will witness cyber wars as a prelude and parallel phenomenon to kinetic wars. This has created uneasiness among nations worldwide, especially those with highly cyber-dependent economies. For Northeast Asia, this holds not only for Japan, South Korea, and Taiwan (Western allies in support of Ukraine) but also for China and North Korea. While the West-oriented trio worries about being targeted by the eastern trio of Russia, China, and North Korea, it can be argued that insecurities against hostile Western intentions instilled in the Eastern nations over a long period has led them to greatly enhance their cyber capabilities. This can potentially create a new regional security dilemma in the cyber domain (a cyber-security fix). To understand the various aspects of how the near future will be shaped for (and in) Northeast Asia, it is vital to analyse the geopolitical dynamics of the nations in the region and their cyber dependence, cyber strategies, and cyber diplomacy. With every country having high stakes in the rapidly evolving cyber-age, observing the regional response in this domain is imperative.

Key words: *Cyber, cybersecurity, cyberattacks, cyberspace, conflict*

Introduction

With the onset of the Russia-Ukraine war, global attention has shifted to Eurasia in 2022. While it may seem that the Northeast Asia (NEA) region remains untouched from significant disturbances resulting from the ongoing war, it is far from so. NEA's regional geopolitical and geo-strategic situation remains in flux; with all the state actors entangled in territorial disputes, historical grievances, non-proliferation concerns, economic inter-dependency, and existential security dilemmas,[1] the war will have multi-fold effects on regional dynamics.

There are several characteristics that make NEA unique in global affairs. The region leads in technological innovation, witnesses high national military expenditures, high rates of Foreign Direct Investments (FDIs), high regional trade, and enviable importance for global supply chains.[2] With matured technological industries like electronics, automobiles, telecommunications, and semiconductors, NEA nations possess high rates of expertise in information technology. At the same time, the region battles realities like hydrocarbon and raw material shortages, and asymmetric economic engagement, resulting in dependency on extra-regional partners.

Currently, China stands as the top trade partner (both import and export) for all the NEA nations (as well as for the Russian Far East region), thereby positioning it as the most significant geo-economic player in the area.[3] This asymmetric gradually spilt over into the political, socio-cultural and security domains, making the NEA nations prone to pressures from Beijing when it comes to China, regarding the ongoing geopolitical competition for global supremacy against the USA. As the region moves toward becoming an arena of competition between the West and the East, any and every, accomplishment leads to bragging rights.

The NEA region is also unique in the absence of regional institutional structures for engagement in security and development-related aspects. Unlike many other areas (Latin America, Central Asia, and Southeast Asia), NEA does not have peace agreements or multilateral mechanisms to discuss common concerns.[4] Instead, the governments primarily engage on bilateral levels on a list of disputes—China's ambitions to reunify Taiwan with the mainland, North Korea's rogue activities for attaining nuclear deterrence, Japan and Russia over the Kuril Islands, South Korea and Japan over historical grievances regarding war crimes, and other disputes and concerns over China's increasing ambitions and aggression in the South and East China Sea.

This situation is further complicated by an expanding competition in the broader Indo-Pacific region,[5] where the Western allies are looking to counter Russian and Chinese attempts to expand militarily, economically, politically, or diplomatically. This was visible in the recent alliance and groupings like the AUKUS (Australia-UK-USA) and the QUAD (India, USA, Japan, Australia).[6] Invariably, this too will have significant implications for the NEA region's overall security and political situation.[7]

The Cyber Scenario

It is believed that every nation seeks to achieve three strategic goals for securing itself—national security, economic growth, and human development.[8] Inability or an imbalance in attaining these goals can lead to undesired concerns. This imbalance is nowhere more visible in the NEA than in the cyber domain. While the NEA economies are vital for global cyberspace because of their innovation and technological advancement emerging from this region, the lack of mechanisms for governmental engagement and cooperation on cyber security and cyber diplomacy makes the region vulnerable to cyber conflicts, cybercrime, and cyber warfare in events of misunderstandings and escalations.

NEA's regional security discussions often revolve around the existential threats emerging from the fears of nuclear proliferation and warfare. With three nuclear-armed nations (Russia, China, and North Korea) motivated by converging interests against the West (even more so with the onset of the Russia-Ukraine war), the other three (South Korea, Taiwan, and Japan) would feel increasingly uneasy over the unfolding situation. For the security and stability of any region today, the nuclear aspect is not the only critical element any more.

Cyberspace is now fundamental to any nation's economic, military, and human development.[9] And as essentialities produce vulnerabilities, challenges for securing national interests in the cyber domain are becoming more visible daily. Today, federal, and industrial leaders are focused on challenges like organised and sophisticated cyber attacks, interference in electoral processes, manipulation of the citizenry through social media, threats to critical infrastructural assets, and loss of intellectual property to cyber theft and espionage.

Keeping an eye on these realities, this chapter aims to understand and highlight the intricacies of the geopolitical landscape of the NEA region in the cyber domain. It delves into how the regional disputes, historical grievances, existential threats, and constitutional limitations are shaping the cyber policies and strategies for Japan, Taiwan, and the

Koreas. Further, this chapter looks into the effects of external factors (like the USA's policies, ambitions, and strategies for the region) in the cyber realm and how the Russia-Ukraine war will impact the NEA.

North Korea: David or Goliath?

Imagining life in North Korea (officially the Democratic People's Republic of Korea) often brings to mind large-scale poverty, hunger, absence of free speech, inaccessibility to knowledge about global developments, and backwardness in technology and innovation.[10] While this image might closely resemble the ground situation, there is one area where North Korea is not to be taken lightly—cyberspace.

According to the USA-based cyber security firm, 'Recorded Future', cyberspace is not simply a fascination or leisure activity. Still, it is a critical tool for revenue generation for the North Korean regime.[11] With a minuscule number of users, the accessibility to cyberspace remains limited to a selected few in North Korea. These are either trusted members of the ruling class or the regime's cyber warriors (estimated to be around 7,000 in number and working from around the world).[12] Even with its modest cyber infrastructure and resource base, Pyongyang has time and again succeeded in bewildering the globe with its feats in the cyber realm. It is believed that North Korea has developed advanced cyber warfare prowess surpassed by only a few nations.[13] Success stories about North Korea's cyber heists, cyber thefts, and other cybercrimes, spanning over a decade, provide a relatively good indication of this cyber prowess.

The first attacks from North Korean hacker groups emerged in 2009 when multiple Distributed-Denial-of-Service attacks rattled South Korean government websites. Since then, different North Korean hacker groups (now categorised as Advanced Persistent Threats or APTs) have attacked South Korea's financial institutions and public broadcasters in 2011 (e.g., destruction of Nonghyup Bank's servers) and in 2013 ('Dark Seoul Attack'), targeted the Korea Hydro and Nuclear Power (South Korea's nuclear power plant operator) to obtain worker details, electricity flow charts, designs and manuals for reactors among other information in 2014, performed financial gain attacks on South Korea's crypto currency exchange institutions and breached computers of the South Korean Ministry of Defence's Acquisition Program Administration to steal plans for South Korea's next-generation fighter aircraft and arms procurement in 2018.[14]

The list does not end at victories against South Korean targets. North Korean hacker groups were reportedly involved in the attack on Sony Pictures in 2014 (forcing the studio to cancel the screening of a movie depicting North Korean Premier Kim Jong-un); an 81-million USD cyber heist from the Central Bank of Bangladesh in 2016; the 'WannaCry' Ransomware attack that wreaked havoc worldwide and halted the UK National Health Service's accident and emergency departments in 2017; espionage attempts on Indian Space Research Organisation (ISRO) and cyber theft attempt on India's Kudankulam nuclear plant for obtaining information on thorium-based power plants in 2019; and several hacking attempts into companies involved in COVID-19 vaccine research and development between 2020 and 2021.[15]

Kim Jong-un has reportedly said, "Cyber warfare is an all-purpose word that guarantees North Korean People's Armed Forces ruthless striking capability, along with nuclear weapons and missiles".[16] While the above success stories give us a glimpse of North Korea's cyber capabilities, the reasons for the Kim regime's emphasis on establishing these cyber capabilities are associated with developing nuclear capabilities for deterrence against the West, especially the USA. To this aim, cyber prowess provides North Korea with a way to finance its ambitions and bypass the isolation and sanctions that have been imposed on the nation since the 1990s.

It is now widely accepted that North Korea receives support from China (and Russia, to some extent) in acquiring skills and capabilities for its cyber warriors and infrastructural capacities. North Korean students often study abroad in top science and technology universities (like the Harbin Institute of Technology in China) and gain access to equipment and technology unavailable back home.[17] North Korea also pursues official academic partnerships with the Chinese government for its universities and plugs into the internet through Russian and Chinese telecom companies. North Korean hacker groups have reportedly engaged in conducting cyber-attacks while residing in hotels in Southeast Asia, China, and nations in East Europe.[18,19]

In some assessments, North Korea is one of the greatest cyber threats capable of launching disruptive or destructive cyber-attacks and makes as much as USD 1 billion in gains from cyber heists every year (a third of North Korea's exports). The nation has evolved from conducting simple DDoS attacks to possessing disruptive cyber capabilities in one decade. As the Russia-Ukraine war brings back the importance of nuclear deterrence to the fore of global geopolitics, North Korea's cyber offensive campaigns can be expected to have a direct impact.

It has been widely argued that the war would have never happened if Ukraine had not renounced its nuclear capabilities in the aftermath of the Soviet dissolution (or if it would have re-attained them later on).[20] For Kim Jong-un, the war provides a golden ticket for continuing its missile tests and silencing critics who might have argued against the Kim regime's unidirectional focus on nuclear capabilities.

The war can lead to two possibilities for North Korea's cyber strategy:

1. Reduced reliance.
2. Increased emphasis.

As Russia would seek markets for expanding its energy exports beyond Europe, North Korea may become one of the beneficiaries of this new development and seek partnerships for trade. For example, with the UN sanctions on North Korea, the oil import cap (500,000 barrels per year) on the nation remains a hindrance to more Russian exports to North Korea.[21] Considering that North Korea was one of the few countries to have voted in favour of Russia on UN resolutions related to the Russia-Ukraine war,[22] if the Russian leadership decides to take a step back from sanctions on North Korea, the ruling regime can look to rejuvenate traditional sectors of the economy like agricultural production and industrial output. North Korea may find the conventional means of earning revenue much more convenient than cyber heists and frauds.

However, in the light of the increased significance of possessing nuclear deterrence capabilities, Kim Jong-un might want to put his revenue earning qualifications in the highest gear and utilise all means possible to position his country as a powerful nuclear-armed nation as soon as possible. This would mean a doubling down on its cyber offensive campaign. In this situation, as the Western partners will look to encircle and pressurise Moscow, Beijing, and Pyongyang, the cyber realm would become a significant avenue to retaliate against the three eastern neighbours.

This raises the question of whether North Korea will remain the underdog in cyberspace (the cyber-David) or will now embark on a journey to become the cyber-Goliath, boosted by a newfound zeal to obtain nuclear capabilities and increased opportunities to pour investments into its cyber capabilities if its neighbours are continued to be isolated by the West.

Japan: Obstinate or Compliant?

If North Korean capabilities in cyberspace were a surprise, the case for Japan is no different, albeit for the opposite reason. While North Korea has looked to excel in offensive cyber capabilities, Japan stands at the opposite end of the spectrum, betting on strong defensive cyber capabilities. While North Korea is often remarked for being in the top ranks of nations with offensive cyber capabilities, Japanese defensive cyber capabilities leave much to be desired.

It is often highlighted that despite having been a leader in technology and innovation spheres for decades, Japan's considerably lower position in its peers with similar industrial and developmental backgrounds does not do justice to its potential.[23] This is evident in various indexes and reports where Japan finds itself at the bottom of the lists. The 'Cyber Capabilities and National Power' 2021 report by the UK-based International Institute for Strategic Studies (IISS) placed Japan in the lowest category (Tier 3, along with Iran, Indonesia, Malaysia, Vietnam, and India) in an assessment of fifteen countries.[24] The evaluation is based on capabilities in several categories like core cyber-intelligence capability, cyber security and resilience, strategy and doctrine, offensive cyber capability, and global leadership in cyberspace affairs. It also highlights that Japan does not have an official military cyber strategy or doctrine on cyberspace. The assessment remarks were prompted in part by the USA and Australia. Japan is now seeking a more robust cyber posture as it considers the concerns emerging in cyberspace, especially from China, North Korea, and Russia.

'The National Cyber Power Index 2020' by the USA-based Belfer Centre for Science and International Affairs, which seeks to measure the cyber capabilities of thirty countries, shows a similar situation for Japan.[25] Japan remains absent from top positions in almost every category and is placed in the 'Lower Capability and Lower Intent' category, alongside

Egypt, Lithuania, and several others. The report explains that the class includes those not actively developing the capability and intent to project power in cyberspace or have not published sufficient information on their cyber strategy, cyber-attacks attributed to them, or capabilities used to measure cyber power in this study. This reality conflicts with Japan's aim to contribute to regional peace and stability through diplomacy and capacity building.

The Ministry of Foreign Affairs of Japan states that its cyber security diplomacy consists of three pillars—promotion of the rule of law in cyberspace, development of Confidence Building Measures (CBMs) and cooperation on capacity building. To this aim, Japan has bilateral cyber dialogues with eleven countries, the EU, and the ASEAN. Japan created the role of 'Ambassador in Charge' of Cyber Policy way back in 2012, rolled out the first official Cybersecurity Strategy in 2013, created a Cybersecurity Strategic Headquarters under the Cabinet to promote cyber security policies in 2014, the National Centre of Incident Readiness and Strategy for Cybersecurity (NISC) in 2015, and a cyber security policy division in the Ministry of Foreign Affairs in 2016.[26] Japan's Ministry of Economy, Trade, and Industry further launched cyber security training centres in 2017.[27]

However, even until 2020, the Japanese Ministry of Defence's allocated budget for cyber capabilities made up less than 1 per cent of its total defence budget. By 2021,[28] Japan's Self Defence Forces operated with approximately only 400 personnel dedicated to cyber security for Japan's Self Defence Forces (JSDF or SDF) as a whole.[29] Comparing this figure to North Korea's cyber warriors (approximately 7,000) is bound to raise questions. But why is there such a mismatch in Japan's potential and existing capabilities in the cyber realm?

The answer lies in its post-war pacifist constitutional framework.

A long-standing policy limits Japan's defence spending to 1 per cent of the national GDP. This *effectively* makes investments in cyber security stand at less than 1 per cent of the total defence budget and equivalent to 0.0001 per cent of the national GDP. Also, Articles 9 and 21 of the constitution prevent the JSDF from engaging in domestic surveillance or conducting pre-emptive warfare,[30,31] thus, neutralising opportunities for defence through cyber offence and forcing Japan to focus on developing solely defensive cyber capabilities. The issue was given some attention in 2015 under former Prime Minister Shinzo Abe when Japan embarked on developing its defence policy in cyberspace.[32] Japan sought to adopt a more active strategic stance since adopting the 2018 defence strategy, but its vulnerabilities in the cyber domain remain multi-fold.[33]

Beyond the nuclear and cyber threats from North Korea, Japan stands at risks posed by China and Russia, primarily when Tokyo seeks to stand with Washington and the European partners on global issues. Japanese companies are reportedly vulnerable to cyber threats from compromised technology components from China embedded within Japan's hardware and software supply chains.[34] Further, there are risks associated with Chinese nationals working and studying in Japanese institutions. Over the last few years, Japan has witnessed a drastic increase in ransomware attacks. In June 2020, a ransomware attack on the automobile giant Honda disrupted its global operations, and in November 2020, a hefty ransom demand shook Capcom—a famous Japanese video game company.[35]

According to a 2018 global survey (by the Washington-based Pew Research Centre) on how societies viewed and ranked risks, it was highlighted that Japanese public opinion considers cyber-attacks a more urgent threat than climate change, the North Korean nuclear program, or the rise of China.[36] It stressed that 71 per cent of Japanese society opines cyber threats as Japan's number one threat in recent years. This has led Tokyo to seek a more robust relationship with Washington and conduct cyber security exchanges with other nations. This is visible in Tokyo's efforts to cooperate on cyber security with its QUAD partners and others like Israel, who have achieved expertise in cyber matters.

The new administration of PM Kishida Fumio introduced the concept of 'diplomacy anchored in realism for the new era' at the start of 2022.[37] He emphasised that coming times will test the resiliency of Japanese diplomacy against the pressures emerging in the region. The Russia-Ukraine war has made sure that these words turn into reality sooner than later.

Though Japan has still sought to maintain its stakes in energy projects in Russia, the hopes that were surviving somehow under the Abe government for reconciliation over the long-standing dispute with Russia on the Kuril islands (or Northern Territories) dispute have now surely evaporated. Unlike in 2014, when Tokyo just placed token sanctions in the aftermath of the conflict in Crimea and escaped the Western pressure to do more, the Kishida government has stood firm with its allies in 2022 and imposed heavy sanctions on Russia's financial institutions and individuals. Russia, pulling out from the already stalled peace talks in March 2022, has proved the same.[38]

Japan now stands at a crossroads in deciding its strategic policy for cyberspace. The question remains whether to continue compliance with the constitutional defensive stance and focus only on cyber defence capabilities or adopt a more active approach and seek capabilities like surveillance, attribution, and functional operations in an adversary's cyberspace to neutralise possibilities of future disruptions. This will need Japan to reform its foundational strategic frameworks (much like how a makeover is expected for the German foreign and military policies in the light of the Russia-Ukraine war).[39]

But Japan will want to avoid compliance to be deemed its obstinacy, at least in cyberspace.

For Japan, the changes forced upon it by the Russia-Ukraine war may not be as dramatic as for its European partners. Despite an escalated cyber threat environment in Japan and an increased number of cyber-attacks attributed to Russian-linked groups (for instance, Toyota decided to shut plants across Japan, fearing cyber-attacks from Russia for reprisals after Japan joined G7 nations in applying tougher sanctions),[40] Japan's major threat will stay rooted in its regional adversary—China.

Before understanding how Beijing affects the regional cyber dynamics, it is pertinent to look at another regional actor who should probably be regarded as NEA's cyber-David.

Taiwan: Urgency and Resilience

In geopolitics, not just regional but global as well, Taiwan (officially the Republic of China or ROC) holds a significant place.[41] Situated just a little more than a hundred miles from the southeastern coast of mainland China, self-governing Taiwan is a critical strategic partner for the West. Taiwan's capabilities in technological innovation and an adherence to democratic virtues in its political system make it an essential geopolitical actor in a region dominated by a rising and authoritarian China (officially People's Republic of China or PRC). Beyond Taiwan's importance in the Western concept of the Indo-Pacific to counterbalance China, Taiwan is emerging as a valuable partner for cooperation in cyber-resilience, countering disinformation, enhancing cyber security, and understanding cyber-threats from China.[42]

The Taiwanese capacity in these domains is invariably linked to its heightened vulnerability against cyber threats, considering that Taiwan and China have a shared language, a level of socio-economic integration, and the long-standing aim of the PRC to unify the ROC by merging it with the mainland.[43] Towards this aim, disinformation and cyber-attacks are now critical elements of the PRC strategy to influence Taiwanese society. The island-nation faces about 30 million cyber-attacks every month, almost half of which originate from China.[44]

Taiwanese efforts to counter the cyber threats emerging from the PRC have been visible since the turn of the century when the government formed the 'National Information and Communication Security Taskforce' in 2001 as an inter-agency body to promote government attention to information security.[45] In the same year, the 'National Centre for Cybersecurity Technology' (NCCST) was created to provide technical services for pre, during, and post-cyber incident activities.[46]

As the threats increased in the previous decade, governmental activity and determination in this domain also accelerated. In 2016, Taiwan established the Department of Cyber Security to improve the implementation of information security measures and delegate responsibilities.[47] Realising the threats to Taiwan's military after numerous cyber-attacks, Taiwan formally established the 'Information, Communication and Electronic Force' (ICEF) Command in 2017 as its cyber warfare unit to serve as the fourth branch of its armed forces.[48] This was the first such independent military cyber command in the world at that time.

The government further amended the National Security Act in 2019 and delineated cyber security as a new part of national security, including cyberspace and physical space within Taiwan's defensible territory. More recently, in 2021, the Taiwan government rolled out the Information Security Strategy 2.0, which seeks to go beyond increased defences and aims to foster closer collaboration between the government, the private sector, and society.[49]

Going beyond policymaking, Taiwan has established an extensive cyber security framework, encompassing legal efforts for ensuring nationwide cyber security standards and operational steps toward cyber defence. Taiwan has sought to create a demand-driven industrial environment for cyber security companies, establish cyber security infrastructure to facilitate maturity in cyberspace governance, achieve a united cyber security system, increase the national cyber security workforce and create a thousand-person response team in government agencies while nurturing talent by providing specialised courses and programmes on cyber security in universities.[50] For Taiwan, cyber security is deemed one the most critical core strategic industries in its 'Five-plus-two' innovative industries plan, which covers sectors like intelligent machinery, national defence, and aerospace.[51]

According to the head of Taiwan's Department of Cybersecurity, Taiwan's critical infrastructure, such as gas, water, and electricity, are now highly digitised.[52] This presents a vulnerability where a cyber-attack able to penetrate the cyber defences can wreak havoc and cause catastrophic disarray to the socio-economic functioning of Taiwanese society, potentially leading to political disturbances caused by an environment of disinformation in the community. The Taiwanese government has rolled out initiatives to identify and combat fake news to neutralise this risk. An example is a new school curriculum to spread awareness about fake news and disinformation.[53]

However, Taiwan remains with several challenges and vulnerabilities, restricting it from considering itself secure in the cyber domain. The most significant of these challenges is Taiwan's limitation in international cooperation, policymaking, and information sharing.

Taiwan remains absent from global policymaking under the 'One China Policy' followed by most countries, including the USA. Taiwan is not a part of the UN (even as an observer), and its efforts to pursue partnerships and cooperation with others remains restricted to bilateral frameworks. Benefitting from asymmetric dependencies in economic partnerships, Beijing has been able to keep Taiwan away from substantial multilateral engagements. This now applies to global and regional forums and processes in the cyber domain, hence making Taiwan a unique case where a strong and capable cyber security-focused geopolitical actor remains restricted by complex diplomatic realities and a lack of opportunities for collaboration and cooperation.

Given how the Russia-Ukraine war has shown the inevitability of all future wars to have a cyber component (thus making the concept 'hybrid war' no more a future possibility but a present reality),[54] the situation endows upon Taiwan a new urgency for building its resilience further. Taiwan will seek to monitor the strategies used in the war closely and understand the tactical playbooks at use.

It has been reported that before 2020, Taiwan was already the most exposed nation to disinformation from foreign sources. This situation may worsen as the Xi government in Beijing eyes fulfilling its ambition to take back Taiwan. However, considering that the USA and Europe look at the prospect of sending a solid reply to Moscow to deter Beijing from any aggressive manoeuvres threatening Taiwan, cyberspace might be the grey zone where China might look to express its displeasure.

With the world increasingly vulnerable in the cyber domain, cyber security might be the next industry (after the semiconductor industry). Meanwhile, Taiwan would look to continue strengthening its cyber defences and encouraging the development of its cyber security industry. It provides Taiwan with an avenue for increasing its global partnerships and presence. By sharing its resilience strategies with other nations lacking cyber defence capacities and a robust cyber defence framework, Taiwan can seek to carve out a more significant role for itself in the global cyber landscape, ultimately contributing to the need for Taiwan's security.

A similar situation where a close adversary poses a significant cyber threat exists in the case of South Korea. But the impact of the Russia-Ukraine war here is much different and expected to be more profound.

South Korea: From a Dove to a Hawk

Complimented as a 'strong internet nation', South Korea (officially, the Republic of Korea or ROK) prides itself on being one of the most wired and innovative nations, with cutting-edge digital technology and an impressive high-speed internet penetration rate. This also makes South Korea vulnerable to attacks in the cyber domain.[55]

As South Korea's peninsular neighbour (North Korea) remains the most aggressive cyber state actor in the world, South Korea's cyber agenda remains occupied with the threats posed by the North Korean cyber offensive campaigns. The Kim regime in Pyongyang has sought to infiltrate and paralyse the Seoul's government's resources and infrastructure, steal secrets, and conduct cyber frauds and heists.

Since facing the first substantial cyber-attacks in 2009, South Korea has taken measures to secure its cyberspace as a priority for national security. Initiating the work on creating a national cyber security strategy in 2009, Seoul established the 'National Cyber Security Masterplan' in 2011, which presented a comprehensive response strategy to deal with cyber threats.[56] In 2014, cyber-attacks were identified as a serious threat in the National Security Strategy, and Seoul scaled up its efforts toward domestic cyber security after that. Seoul appointed a cyber security officer in its National Security Council in 2015 who served as the presidential advisor.

Seoul consolidated its cyber security strategy and rolled out its 'National Cybersecurity Strategy' in 2019, aiming to strengthen the nation's digital infrastructure and stable operations of governmental functions.[57] In a move to provide directions toward achieving concrete measures, the Ministry of Science and Information and Communication Technology, the National Intelligence Service, and the Ministry of National Defence came up with the 'National Cybersecurity Basic Plan' in 2019, which listed a hundred detailed tasks necessary for safeguarding South Korea in an increasingly cyber-dependent world.[58]

But beyond the policymaking efforts and technical capabilities towards cyber security, Seoul has faced dilemmas associated with regional and global politics. Under the Moon Jae-in government, Seoul has maintained a hedging strategy in its foreign policy to balance the expectations and ambitions of its two most important economic and security partners—the USA and China—and avoid escalatory unpleasantness in its relations with Russia and North Korea.[59] The Moon government is said to have been less favourable to sanctioning North Korea and to have adopted a lacklustre approach towards monitoring the UN-imposed sanctions on Pyongyang.

Under Moon's leadership, Seoul has also been criticised for ignoring concerns associated with the rise of China, the Taiwanese security concerns, and the necessity for closely cooperating with emerging alliances (QUAD) to counter increasing Chinese dominance in the region.[60] As China remains South Korea's top trading partner, Seoul has sought to favour industrial and business interests instead of inviting conflict.

Fearing for South Korean trade interests with Russia, it was only after intense pressure from the USA (for instance, threats to nullify trade exemptions needed by South Korea) and South Korean civil society protests that the Moon government decided to stand with its Western partners.[61] This approach was also visible in the first few weeks of the onset of the Russia-Ukraine war. However, unlike in any other case we saw in this chapter, a change in political leadership in South Korea, with Moon Jae-in stepping down and Yoon Suk-yeol taking over the presidency in early May 2022, it is expected that South Korea's regional and global geopolitical perspectives undergo significant transformation.

While Moon Jae-in was considered dovish towards North Korea, China, and Russia, Yoon Suk-yeol is expected to take a hawkish approach and favour bringing Seoul closer to its Western partners.[62] In contrast to the Moon government, which avoided agreeing to substantial support for Ukraine, the new government in Seoul is expected to reverse this inclination and work towards decreasing South Korea's dependency on Russia and China. Yoon has emphasised the importance of posing a strong deterrence against North Korea and has defined it as South Korea's main enemy.[63]

This is in stark contrast to South Korea's cyber security strategies under the Moon government, which avoided any explicit mention to prevent possibilities of de-engagement with Pyongyang. It is speculated that the Yoon government will look at bolstering South Korea's military capabilities and might seek a reset in ties with China. It should not be surprising that this involves numerous possibilities for a regional arms race to emerge. And given how the absence of a nuclear deterrent has given a stimulant to the Kim regime's nuclear ambitions, it would not be far-fetched to say that South Korea might be wondering about its deterrent capabilities beyond the protection assured by Washington.[64]

This is where things might spill over in cyber space's grey and often 'lawless' zone. Every move to take South Korea closer to the West can antagonise Beijing and Moscow. While diplomatic expressions of displeasure and conventional methods of pressuring Seoul into maintaining the status quo would be on display, the NEA region might turn into a cyber battleground.

The Quest for Cyber Superiority: USA, China, and Russia

As the world's top military power and the only Tier 1 cyber power in most assessments, the impact that the USA will have on the emerging cyber era cannot be ignored. The USA has become inseparable from discussions over any regional strategic and security discourse in the NEA region due to its long-standing and substantial military, economic, political, and geopolitical engagement with allies like South Korea and Japan.

The USA-Japan-South Korea trilateral alliance was first established by the USA, aimed at containing the Soviet Union, and relied on these nations' aggregated resources and synergies when working in concert.[65] But historical grievances and disputes over issues like reparations related to sexual slavery, forced labour, and human rights abuses during Japan's colonial rule and wartime administration of Korea have led to strained Japan-South Korea ties[66] in recent years and a weaker trilateral alliance overall. Under the Trump Administration, the US government followed a hands-off approach toward tensions between its two allies.[67] Much has changed now, and more changes can be expected ahead. With a change in leadership in each of the three nations (Biden 2021, Kishida 2021, Yoon in May 2022), the dynamics of the alliance can undergo a tectonic shift in the light of the Russia-Ukraine war. A more multilateralism-oriented president in the USA and one in South Korea looking to ally with the West to counter North Korea and China seem like the dynamic lacking in recent times to pull the USA-led alliance together.

Standing against this alliance will be the two Asian cyber giants—China and Russia (Figure 3.1). The three nations have intended to use cyber to achieve policy goals and have infused substantial investments and efforts to achieve the capabilities needed to pursue their policy goals. The Belfer Centre's National Cyber Power Index highlights that while the USA leads in surveillance objectives, information control, and intelligence, Russia tops the list regarding offence capabilities, and China takes the podium in cyber defence capabilities. China leads in intent to realise commercial objectives in the cyber domain, while Russia tops the intent in surveillance.

Again, this is highlighted by the IISS's 'Cyber Capabilities and National Power Assessment', where China is reported to have an established framework for a multi-stakeholder approach to cyber governance (although with the Chinese Communist Party (CCP) as the dominant stakeholder).[68] The assessment notes that while many states today have substantial cyber capabilities and regional intelligence footprint, few have sufficient reach to achieve the qualifications necessary for conducting sophisticated cyber operations. China, Russia, and the USA find place in this category. Another report by the IISS notes that these three nations have dedicated roughly the same proportion of forces to conducting cyber intelligence, surveillance, and reconnaissance (between 50 and 54 per cent).[69]

Figure 3.1: The Two blocs in Cyberspace in Northeast Asia

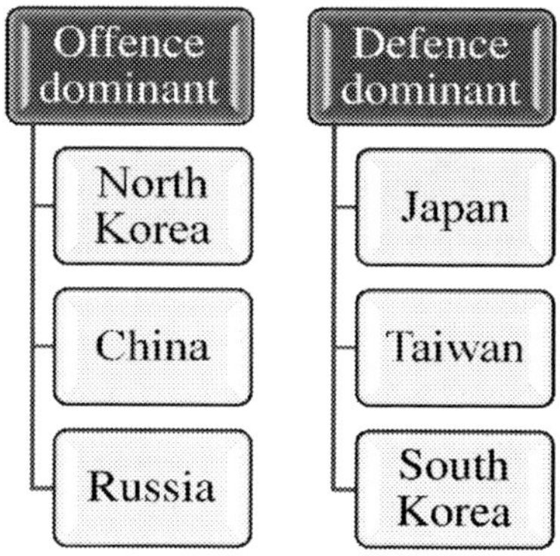

Most experts agree that, for now, only China can catch up with the USA in the coming years in terms of military superiority. The same might not be accurate in the cyber world. Though the USA remains the leader in cyber capabilities and abilities to carry out national objectives through cyber, China continues to build upon its cyber strength. As China aims to become the leading Artificial Intelligence (AI) superpower by 2030, Beijing is leaving no stone unturned in investments and information-gathering aspects.[70]

While consistently denying having conducted state-sponsored hacking or targeted foreign organisations with cyber-attacks, China continues to rattle the world with its commercially motivated cyber espionage and politically motivated cyber-attacks. This happens to the extent that China is now regularly alleged to have been conducting industrial espionage and endowing substantial advantages to its domestic industries to enable them to compete against and outperform competition from the Western tech giants.[71] It is speculated that China has dedicated information-warfare militia units in place,[72] responsible for identifying and launching offensive missions and intelligence gathering (e.g., the third and fourth departments of the General Staff Department of the People's Liberation Army).

The three cyber giants are also embroiled in a battle over norms of behaviour and the scope and nature of applicability of international law in the cyber domain. Much like the Cold War era, the world is currently divided into two blocs regarding cyberspace governance.[73] The USA and the EU-led bloc emphasises the free flow of data in cyberspace, the applicability of existing international law to the full extent in cyberspace, and the freedom to access the internet unimpeded for all.

On the other hand, the China and Russia-led bloc places importance on the sovereign ability to control the information space and on negotiating a new set of laws and norms that would be much more conducive for the cyber domain. The two approaches are categorised as 'cyber security' (meant to protect against attacks in cyberspace) and 'information security' (intended to protect data from any form of threat, within or beyond cyberspace, including the influence of data manipulation on the mind and emotions of the consumer) (Figure 3.2).

Moreover, as Beijing seeks to counter the long-standing Western supremacy in technological innovation through substantial investments in diplomatic, human resources and infrastructure building efforts like the Digital Silk Road, another race between China and the USA—to dominate the global supply chains of information technology resources and an overpowering digital-industrial capacity—is taking place.[74] This, too, can divide the world between allies and adversaries.

Figure 3.2: The two approaches toward security in the cyber domain

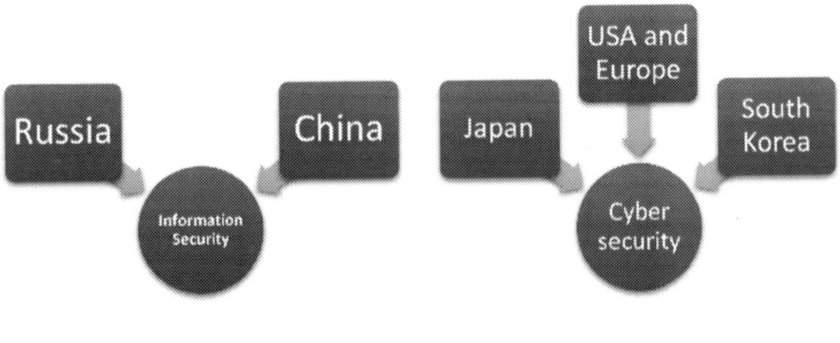

The Russia-Ukraine war is expected to further accelerate this quest for supremacy. Though China has remained officially neutral and has called for a peaceful solution, it is not a mystery to understand where Beijing's interests are. As Russia's economic relationships with Europe worsen, it will be China that stands to gain the most, with Moscow now seeking to widen markets for its hydrocarbon and other resource exports and being forced to do away with Western-technological solutions in cyber security, banking, and public services.

What Lies Ahead?

Considering the dynamics highlighted in this chapter, it seems inevitable that competition and conflict (2Cs) in the cyber domain will intensify in the NEA region in the decade ahead. But there remains a possibility of a '3C' model, where cooperation in maintaining peace in cyberspace can be mutually agreed upon as a confidence-building measure and as a first step to bridge differences and disputes. While this model is unreliable for North Korea, as the Kim regime looks on course to maintain its position as an outlier in global affairs and will focus on its nuclear deterrence ambitions, this model can work between China, Russia, Taiwan, and the Koreas.

The change in the South Korean presidency is expected to result in Seoul's increased cooperation with the Western allies while decoupling from China, possibly resulting in conflict and competition. Taiwan will look to bolster its cyber defences and resilience by cooperating with its Western partners and competing for more outstanding cyber security capabilities than its political nemesis across the Strait.

Taiwan's expertise can be helpful for Japan and South Korea as they seek to strengthen their defences against adversaries, especially China and North Korea. The USA will again look to sew the USA-South Korea-Japan alliance together and hope to engage with the new governments in both Tokyo and Seoul with a call to come together at a time when Western democratic and sovereign values are under attack.

As the sanctions force Russia to look for new partners in the east and beyond Europe, it might be a perfect opportunity for the Kim regime to come out of its recent isolation and find some relief in Moscow's expedition. Cooperation in cyberspace between this eastern trio, coordination between the Western trio, and a sense of rising competition and conflict among the two trios might be a recipe for both exploitation of cyberspace as the grey zone of future disputes and as a starting point to construct in effect a demilitarised area for confidence building. This situation might spill over into debates on cyberspace governance and norm building processes on platforms like the UN, with the regional state actors starkly divided on the two principles.

Overall, the NEA region is expected to remain a frontrunner in technological innovation and capabilities, but this will bring higher vulnerabilities too. In the new cyber era, the 3Cs—Competition, Conflict and Cooperation—will be significant for NEA.

ENDNOTES

1. Andrey Kortunov (2021), "Security and Development in Northeast Asia: New Approaches Needed," *Russian International Affairs Council*, URL: https://russiancouncil.ru/en/analytics-and-comments/analytics/security-and-development-in-northeast-asia-new-approaches-needed/ , accessed on April 27, 2022.
2. Ibid.
3. "Economic Statistics for the Countries of Northeast Asia," The Economic Research Institute for Northeast Asia, March 2021, https://www.erina.or.jp/en/data/asia/economic_statistics/.
4. James Goodby and Markku Heiskanen (2021), "Toward an Organization for Security and Cooperation in Northeast Asia," Asia-Pacific Leadership Network, URL: https://www.apln.network/analysis/commentaries/toward-an-organization-for-security-and-cooperation-in-northeast-asia, accessed on April 29, 2022.
5. Shruti Pandalai (2021), "Emerging Trends in Indo-Pacific Geopolitics: Navigating the 'India Way'" Observer Research Foundation, URL: https://www.orfonline.org/expert-speak/emerging-trends-in-indo-pacific-geopolitics-navigating-the-india-way/, accessed on May 02, 2022.
6. Akshobh Giridhardas (2021), "Why the AUKUS Helps the Quad?" Observer Research Foundation, , URL: https://www.orfonline.org/expert-speak/why-the-aukus-helps-the-quad/, accessed on May 2, 2022.
7. Peter Hayes, "The Future of a Nuclear Weapons-Free Northeast Asia" in *The Future of East Asia*, ed. Chung-in Moon, *Asia Today* (Singapore: Springer, 2018), 227–66, https://doi.org/10.1007/978-981-10-4977-4_9
8. Kortunov (2021), "Security and Development in Northeast Asia: New Approaches Needed".
9. S.D. Pradhan (2021), "Japan's New Cyber Security Strategy: Significant Dimensions" *The Times of India*, URL: https://timesofindia.indiatimes.com/blogs/ChanakyaCode/japans-new-cyber-security-strategy-significant-dimensions/, accessed on May 03, 2022.

10. *Liberty In North Korea* (2022), "The North Korean People's Challenges", URL: https://www.libertyinnorthkorea.org/learn-nk-challenges, accessed on May 04, 2022.
11. *Recorded Future Insikt Group* (2020) "How North Korea Revolutionized the Internet as a Tool for Rogue Regimes" URL: https://www.recordedfuture.com/north-korea-internet-tool/, accessed on May 04, 2022.
12. Priscilla Moriuchi (2018), "North Korea's Ruling Elite Adapt Internet Behavior to Foreign Scrutiny" *Recorded Future,* URL: https://www.recordedfuture.com/north-korea-internet-behavior/, accessed on May 05, 2022.
13. Kim Min-hyung, "North Korea's Cyber Capabilities and Their Implications for International Security" *Sustainability* 14, no. 3 (2022): 1744, https://doi.org/10.3390/su14031744
14. "Significant Cyber Incidents, Centre for Strategic and International Studies" accessed September 16, 2021, https://www.csis.org/programs/strategic-technologies-program/significant-cyber-incidents.
15. *Recorded Future Insikt Group* (2022) "North Korea Cyber Activity", URL: https://go.recordedfuture.com/hubfs/reports/north-korea-activity.pdf, accessed on May 05, 2022.
16. Bruce Klingner (2021), "North Korea", *The Heritage Foundation,* URL: https://www.heritage.org/military-strength/assessing-threats-us-vital-interests/north-korea, accessed on May 06, 2022.
17. Jason Bartlett (2020), "Why Is North Korea So Good at Cybercrime?" *The Diplomat,* URL: https://thediplomat.com/2020/11/why-is-north-korea-so-good-at-cybercrime/, accessed on May 2, 2022.
18. Jason Bartlett (2021), "New Rule From US Commerce May Help Limit Spread of North Korean Cybercrime", *The Diplomat,* URL: https://thediplomat.com/2021/10/new-rule-from-us-commerce-may-help-limit-spread-of-north-korean-cybercrime/, accessed on May 4, 2022.
19. Jason Bartlett (2020), "Exposing the Financial Footprints of North Korea's Hackers" *Centre for New American Security,* URL: https://www.cnas.org/publications/reports/exposing-the-financial-footprints-of-north-koreas-hackers, accessed on May 1, 2022.
20. Mary Louise Kelly and Kat Lonsdorf (2022), "Why Ukraine Gave up Its Nuclear Weapons — and What That Means in an Invasion by Russia" *National Public Radio,* URL: https://www.npr.org/2022/02/21/1082124528/ukraine-russia-putin-invasion, accessed on May 1, 2022.
21. *Nikkei Asia* (2020), "North Korea Accused of Breaching UN Oil Import Limits - Nikkei Asia", URL: https://asia.nikkei.com/Politics/International-relations/North-Korea-accused-of-breaching-UN-oil-import-limits, accessed on May 1, 2022.
22. Chaewon Chung and Arius Derr (2022), "North Korea Votes against UN Resolution Condemning Russia's Invasion of Ukraine" *North Korea News,* URL: https://www.nknews.org/2022/03/north-korea-votes-against-un-resolution-condemning-russias-invasion-of-ukraine/, accessed on May 4, 2022.
23. Junno Kobara (2021), "High-Tech Japan at Bottom of Global 'cyber Power' Rankings: Study" *Nikkei Asia,* URL: https://asia.nikkei.com/Business/Technology/High-tech-Japan-at-bottom-of-global-cyber-power-rankings-study, accessed on May 5, 2022.
24. *The International Institute for Strategic Studies* (2021), "Cyber Capabilities and National Power: A Net Assessment", URL: https://www.iiss.org/blogs/research-

paper/2021/06/cyber-capabilities-national-power, accessed on May 6, 2022.

25. Voo, Julia, Irfan Hemani, Simon Jones, Winnona DeSombre, Dan Cassidy, and Anina Schwarzenbach, "National Cyber Power Index 2020", Cambridge: Belfer Centre for Science and International Affairs, 2020.
26. Yuichi Sakaguichi (2021), "Japan Lashes out against Alleged Chinese Military Cyberattacks" *Nikkei Asia*, URL: https://asia.nikkei.com/Business/Technology/Japan-lashes-out-against-alleged-Chinese-military-cyberattacks, accessed on May 7, 2022.
27. Anne Leonore Dardene (2018), "Cybersecurity: The Potential for Japan-India Cooperation – Asia Dialogue" *The Asia Dialogue*, URL: https://theasiadialogue.com/2018/05/30/japanese-cybersecurity-and-the-potential-for-japan-india-cooperation/, accessed on May 08, 2022.
28. Samuel Arnold-Parra (2021), "A Neglected Frontier: Challenges to Japan's Cyber Security", *Global Risk Insights*, URL: https://globalriskinsights.com/2021/01/a-neglected-frontier-challenges-to-japans-cyber-security/, accessed on May 7, 2022.
29. Ibid.
30. Thomas Glucksmann (2021), "How Will Japan's Cybersecurity Posture Impact Its Relations With China?" *The Diplomat*, URL: https://thediplomat.com/2021/10/how-will-japans-cybersecurity-posture-impact-its-relations-with-china/, accessed on May 07, 2022.
31. Benjamin Bartlett, "Japan: An Exclusively Defense-Oriented Cyber Policy" *Asia Policy* 15 (2), 2020, pp. 93–100.
32. Eugenio Benincasa (2020), "A Missing Piece in Japan's Cyber Defense" *The Diplomat*, URL: https://thediplomat.com/2020/11/a-missing-piece-in-japans-cyber-defense/, accessed on May 7, 2022.
33. Ibid.
34. Glucksmann, "How Will Japan's Cybersecurity Posture Impact Its Relations With China?"
35. Thisanka Siripala (2020), "Japanese Companies Fall Victim To Unprecedented Wave of Cyber Attacks" *The Diplomat*, URL: https://thediplomat.com/2020/12/japanese-companies-fall-victim-to-unprecedented-wave-of-cyber-attacks/, accessed on May 7, 2022.
36. Tobias Burgers, Scott N. Romaniuk, and Cherry H.Y. Wong, "Routledge Companion to Global Cyber-Security Strategy" in *Japan's Challenges, Capabilities, and Preparedness in Cyberspace*, Routledge Handbooks Online, 2021.
37. Yuki Tatsumi (2022), "How Russia's Invasion of Ukraine Changed Japan's Security Policy" *The Diplomat*, URL: https://thediplomat.com/2022/03/how-russias-invasion-of-ukraine-changed-japans-security-policy/, accessed on May 8, 2022.
38. *The Hindu* (2022), "Russia Drops Peace Talks with Japan over Ukraine,", URL: https://www.thehindu.com/news/international/russia-drops-peace-talks-with-japan-over-ukraine/article65247111.ece. accessed on May 8, 2022.
39. Oliver Noyan (2022), "Russia's War in Ukraine Triggers U-Turn in Germany's Foreign Policy Thinking" *Euractive*, URL: https://www.euractiv.com/section/europe-s-east/news/russias-war-in-ukraine-triggers-u-turn-in-germanys-foreign-policy-thinking/, accessed on May 08, 2022.
40. Peter Lyon (2022), "Russia Is Suspect In Cyberattack That Will Force Toyota To Shut Down Plants In Japan," *Forbes*, URL: https://www.forbes.com/sites/peterlyon/2022/02/28/russia-is-suspect-in-cyberattack-that-will-force-toyota-to-

shut-down-plants-in-japan/, accessed on May 08, 2022.

41. Ruchir Sharma (2020), "World's Most Important Place: How Tiny Taiwan Came to Be the Epicentre of the Global Battle for Tech Supremacy," *The Times of India*, URL: https://timesofindia.indiatimes.com/blogs/toi-edit-page/worlds-most-important-place-how-tiny-taiwan-came-to-be-the-epicentre-of-the-global-battle-for-tech-supremacy/, accessed on May 08, 2022.
42. Diana Liu (2021), "As EU-Taiwan Ties Deepen, Cybersecurity Is Front and Centre," *France 24*, URL: https://www.france24.com/en/asia-pacific/20211211-as-eu-taiwan-ties-deepen-cybersecurity-is-front-and-centre, accessed on May 08, 2022.
43. Tania Millan et al. (2019), "Perspectives on Taiwan: Insights from the 2018 Taiwan-U.S. Policy Program", *Centre for Strategic & International Studies*, URL: https://rowman.com/ISBN/9781442281097/Perspectives-on-Taiwan-Insights-from-the-2018-Taiwan-U.S.-Policy-Program., accessed on May 09, 2022.
44. Audrey Tang and Joseph Wu (2021), "Why Taiwan Seeks Israel's Help to Combat Cybersecurity Threats" *The Jerusalem Post*, URL: https://www.jpost.com/opinion/why-taiwan-seeks-israels-help-to-combat-cybersecurity-threats-opinion-674983, accessed on May 09, 2022.
45. Millan et al., "Perspectives on Taiwan."
46. Ibid.
47. Ibid.
48. Ibid.
49. Tobias Burgers, Moritz Hellmann, and Scott N. Romaniuk, "In the Line of Fire: Taiwan's Legal, Political, and Technological Cybersecurity Posture," in *Routledge Companion to Global Cyber-Security Strategy, London:* Routledge, 2021.
50. Hsini Huang (2020), "A Collaborative Battle in Cybersecurity? Threats and Opportunities for Taiwan," *Asia Policy* 15(2), pp. 101–106.
51. *Timothy Ferry (2017), "The 5+2 Industrial Innovation Plan" Taiwan Business*, URL: https://topics.amcham.com.tw/2017/05/52-industrial-innovation-plan/, accessed on May 10, 2022.
52. *The New Indian Express* (2021), "Amid China's Military Pressure, Taiwan Prepares for Cyber War," URL: https://www.newindianexpress.com/world/2021/jul/25/amid-chinas-military-pressure-taiwan-prepares-for-cyber-war-2335147.html, accessed on May 10, 2022.
53. Millan et al., "Perspectives on Taiwan."
54. *The New Indian Express* (2022), "Russia-Ukraine Conflict First True Instance of Hybrid Warfare, Has a Lot of Lessons: IAF Chief", URL: https://www.newindianexpress.com/nation/2022/apr/12/russia-ukraine-conflict-first-true-instance-of-hybrid-warfare-has-a-lot-of-lessons-iaf-chief-2441259.html, accessed on May 12, 2022.
55. Yangmo Ku, "An Effective Shield?: Analyzing South Korea's Cybersecurity Strategy" in *Routledge Companion to Global Cyber-Security Strategy*, 1st edn., London: Routledge, 2021.
56. Ibid.
57. Kim So Jeong and Bae Sunha (2021), "Korean Policies of Cybersecurity and Data Resilience - The Korean Way With Data: How the World's Most Wired Country Is Forging a Third Way," *Carnegie Endowment for International Peace*, URL: https://carnegieendowment.org/2021/08/17/korean-policies-of-cybersecurity-and-data-resilience-pub-85164, accessed on May 13, 2022.

58. Ibid.
59. Cheol Hee Park (2019), "Strategic Estrangement between South Korea and Japan as a Barrier to Trilateral Cooperation", *Atlantic Council of the United States,* URL: https://www.atlanticcouncil.org/wp-content/uploads/2019/12/Strategic-Estrangement-Report-web.pdf, accessed on May 13, 2022.
60. Jagannath Panda (2022), "Beyond North Korea: The Japan-South Korea-US Trilateral in the Indo-Pacific" *The Diplomat,* URL: https://thediplomat.com/2022/02/beyond-north-korea-the-japan-south-korea-us-trilateral-in-the-indo-pacific/, accessed on 14, May 2022.
61. Robert Kelly (2022), "South Korea's Bewildering Stance on the Ukraine Conflict" *The Japan Times,* URL: https://www.japantimes.co.jp/opinion/2022/04/18/commentary/world-commentary/south-korea-confusion-ukraine/, accessed May 13, 2022.
62. Andrew Gilholm (2022), "Planning for Geopolitical Flashpoints: A Northeast Asia Perspective," *Control Risks,* URL: https://www.controlrisks.com/our-thinking/insights/planning-for-geopolitical-flashpoints-a-northeast-asia-perspective, accessed on May 13, 2022.
63. Lee Haye-ah (2022), "Yoon Vows to Strengthen Deterrence against N. Korea's Nuclear Missile Threats", *Yonhap News Agency,* URL: https://en.yna.co.kr/view/AEN20220407003454315, accessed on May 14, 2022.
64. Christian Davies (2022), "Nervous South Koreans Seek Ways to Counter North's Nuclear Threat" *Financial Times,* URL: https://www.ft.com/content/b0cf218f-d893-40aa-9994-0d3ce8e4adc5, accessed on May 14, 2022.
65. James Lewis (2015), Cyber Cooperation in Northeast Asia, *The National Bureau of Asian Research,* URL: https://www.nbr.org/publication/cyber-cooperation-in-northeast-asia/, accessed on May 12, 2022.
66. Andrew Park and Elliot Silverberg (2021), "Mutual Suspicion, Mutual Threats: Getting Japan and South Korea to Work Together" *War on the Rocks,* URL: https://warontherocks.com/2021/04/mutual-suspicion-mutual-threats-getting-japan-and-south-korea-to-work-together/, accessed on May 13, 2022.
67. Hwang Joon-bum (2019), "US Adopts Hands-off Approach to S. Korea-Japan Trade Dispute: International" *The Hankyoreh,* URL: http://english.hani.co.kr/arti/english_edition/e_international/901274.html, accessed on May 14, 2022.
68. *International Institute for Strategic Studies,* "Cyber Capabilities and National Power."
69. Mark Pomerleau (2022), "Russia and China Devote More Cyber Forces to Offensive Operations than US, Says New Report," *C4ISRNet,* URL: https://www.c4isrnet.com/cyber/2022/02/14/russia-and-china-devote-more-cyber-forces-to-offensive-operations-than-us-says-new-report/, accessed on May 14, 2022.
70. Joccheim Ulrich (2021), "China's Ambitions in Artificial Intelligence", *European Parliamentary Research Service,* URL: https://www.europarl.europa.eu/RegData/etudes/ATAG/2021/696206/EPRS_ATA(2021)696206_EN.pdf, accessed on May 14, 2022.
71. Sabri Ben-Achour (2021), "China's State-Backed Cyberattacks Are Part of a Larger Plan", *Marketplace,* URL: https://www.marketplace.org/2021/12/09/chinas-state-sponsored-industrial-espionage-is-part-of-a-larger-system/, accessed on May 14, 2022.
72. *Firstpost* (2021) ,"China Strengthening Its Cyberattack Capabilities: What It Means

for India and Regional Peace" URL: https://www.firstpost.com/india/taiwan-says-it-faces-5-mn-cyberattacks-daily-a-look-at-chinas-cyber-capabilities-what-it-means-for-india-10128621.html, accessed on May 14, 2022.

73. James Shires (2018), "Between Multistakeholderism and Sovereignty: Cyber Norms in Egypt and the Gulf States" *Belfer Centre for Science and International Affairs*, URL: https://www.belfercenter.org/publication/between-multistakeholderism-and-sovereignty-cyber-norms-egypt-and-gulf-states, accessed on May 14, 2022.
74. Michael Wolf and Ira Kalish (2021), "Supply Chain Resilience in the Face of Geopolitical Risks," *Deloitte Insights*, URL: https://www2.deloitte.com/us/en/insights/economy/us-china-trade-war-supply-chain.html, accessed on May 14, 2022.

CHAPTER 4

South Korean Diplomacy Amidst Russia's War

Palak Maheshwari

ABSTRACT

South Korea is considered a middle power capable of mediating and influentially contributing to the international arena. This is because it has a large economy, high per capita income, and standard of living, an important position in the Indo-Pacific, and is committed to the international rule of law and multilateralism. This middle power status also comes with expectations of taking a firm stand when faced with a conflict of global proportions like the one unfolding in Ukraine at the present moment.

South Korea's response to the Russia-Ukraine conflict is underlined by its commitments and considerations on two critical fronts; its long-standing conflict with North Korea and its crucial military alliance with the USA. South Korea's decision to join Western-led sanctions against Moscow was a significant departure from its foreign policy in the past. As an export-dependent economy, South Korea has traditionally refused to impose sanctions in cases of conflicts directly. Instead, it has focused on insulating itself economically from the after effects. Even when there were USA-led sanctions during Russia's invasion of Crimea in 2014, South Korea abstained, and chose to maintain economic ties with Moscow. In this chapter, I argue that South Korea's decision to impose sanctions on Russia this time indicates the maturity of South Korea's middle power diplomacy, its status as an alliance partner of the USA and its desire to unequivocally support the inviolability of territorial sovereignty in the face of its regional threat in the North.

Key words: *South Korea, middle power, diplomacy, economic sanctions, Ukraine crisis*

Introduction

On 28 February 2022, South Korea joined the US-led economic sanctions against Russia. This came four days after the Russian invasion of Ukraine. Export of several strategic items like semiconductors, sensors and lasers, marine equipment, and electronics, to Russia was blocked completely. The export of some non-strategic items was closely reviewed.[1] The South Korean government also participated in the exclusion of Russian banks from the SWIFT[2] banking system. It used the Strategic Petroleum Reserve to offset any instability in the global energy market due to this conflict. In coordination with the international community, South Korea also contributed humanitarian assistance to Ukraine.[3]

Regarding international crises that do not directly fall within South Korea's proximity, Seoul has historically not taken such a strong stance. Contrast this with the events of 2014 when Russia invaded Ukraine and took control of the Crimean Territory. In 2014, South Korea seeking to protect its economic interests did not put sanctions against Russia, and only provided the necessary condemnation required to meet its role as an alliance partner of the USA.[4]

What changed between these two instances of Russian aggression? Why was Seoul compelled into action this time? The answer lies in how South Korea sees itself in the international arena and how it perceives its global role. This chapter will argue how the growing South Korean economy, its middle-power status, and its considerations of the North Korean threat informed Seoul's foreign policy actions during Russia's invasion of Ukraine in 2022.

The changing profile of South Korea

A lot has changed for South Korea since 2014. It is a top-ten global economy, was invited as a guest country to the G7 and is increasingly becoming crucial in multilateral institutions of global economic decision-making.[5]

In 2008, in the middle of the global financial crisis, President George W. Bush of the USA convened a meeting of the 20 largest economies of the world, and Seoul won a seat at the table. This grouping, termed the G20, was to act as a 'global economic steering committee.' Middle powers, particularly South Korea, have been able to mediate this grouping on issues of critical importance. South Korea has led discussions on global financial safety nets for the emerging markets and the development of permanent institutions for the G20. This leadership role undertaken by Seoul makes it attractive to both developed and emerging economies. Because the Asian economic powerhouse rose from strategic vulnerability and abject poverty relatively recently, it is seen as a role model for emerging economies, especially in Asia. It is also appreciated as a robust and responsible player (closely allied to the USA, and, in extension, committed to the liberal international order) in the global arena by the developed states.[6] South Korea is also a member of the Organization for Economic Cooperation and Development (OECD), an intergovernmental economic organization committed to democratic ideals and a free market economy.

Traditionally, countries that did not belong to either group of large developed countries or large developing countries were considered middle powers. This qualifies Australia, Canada, Sweden, Norway and other Nordic countries as middle powers. But now, countries such as South Korea, Turkey and Mexico are also self-identifying and taking on characteristics of middle powers. This is crucial because these countries add the dimension of responsible global leadership and mediation to the definition of middle powers:

> 'These new middle powers are upper-income or upper-middle-income developing countries whose national interests in global governance are beginning to diverge from those of large, relatively low-income developing countries due to their successful economic and political development. More so than other developing countries, middle power developing countries are more likely to assume global responsibilities and have greater faith in the capacity of developing countries for successful development.'[7]

With the tag of being a middle power also comes the expectation of taking strong stances on issues of global importance and the responsibility to safeguard international norms such as the inviolability of territorial borders.[8] Scholars of the constructivist school of thought of international politics would also argue that when a country's international profile increases, there is also an expectation from the domestic public to become a vanguard with other global leaders and spearhead efforts to uphold international norms. South Korea's self-perception has drastically changed from the twentieth to the twenty-first century due to its high income and industrialization. If a state's self-perception is known, it is easy to predict its behaviour in the international system. 'A particular role that a state assigns to itself in the international system is an important variable in defining the state's national interest and how it will use its available material resources of power to its advantage.'[9] The country's self-perception is not limited to its state machinery; it is also closely linked to the domestic population's imagination.

South Korea's ability to affect decision-making, significant expansion of multilateral economic diplomacy, and emergence as a key leader in development assistance for emerging countries have set a solid basis for Seoul's middle power status. Table 4.1 (below) lists Seoul's achievements in global diplomacy until right before the Russian invasion of Crimea in 2014.

Table 4.1: South Korea's Global Diplomacy

Year	*Event*
December 1948	The United Nations General Assembly recognizes the Republic of Korea
25 June 1950	The Korean War breaks out
July 1950	The United Nations Security Council votes to authorize United Nations members to provide military forces to the Republic of Korea
July 1953	The Korean Armistice Agreement takes effect
August 1955	South Korea becomes a member of the International Monetary Fund and the World Bank
July 1964	The South Korean National Assembly authorizes the deployment of Korean troops in Vietnam
March 1967	South Korea accedes to the General Agreements on Tariffs and Trade
April 1975	South Korea becomes a signatory to the Nuclear Non-Proliferation Treaty
September 1981	The International Olympic Committee awards the 1988 Summer Olympic Games to Seoul, Korea
September 1988	Seoul hosts the 24th Summer Olympic Games
April 1991	The South Korean government sets up a new development assistance agency, the Korea International Cooperation Agency (KOICA)
September 1991	The United Nations General Assembly votes to admit South Korea as a member country along with North Korea
July 1993	South Korean peacekeeping troops arrive in Somalia, the first time South Korea participated in United Nations peacekeeping operations

Year	*Event*
November 1995	South Korea was elected to the United Nations Security Council for a two-year term (1996-1997)
December 1996	South Korea joins the OECD
November 1997	The South Korean government asks the IMF for a stand-by loan in a worsening currency crisis
June 2001	South Korean foreign minister Han Seung-soo is elected to the presidency of the United Nations General Assembly
November 2001	South Korea is elected for the first time to the Executive Board of the IMF for one term (2003-2005)
May 2003	The World Health Assembly appoints Dr. Jong-wook Lee as the director-general of the World Health Organization
October 2005	South Korean foreign minister Ban Ki-moon elected United Nations secretary-general for a five-year term (2006-2011)
February 2008	President Lee Myung-bak is inaugurated as the 17th president of the Republic of Korea
July 2008	President Lee participates in the G8 Toyako Summit at the invitation of the Japanese government
October 2008	Bank of Korea and the Federal Reserve Board establish reciprocal currency arrangements (swap lines)
November 2008	The USA invites South Korea to the first G20 summit in Washington
November 2009	South Korea accedes to the OECD Development Assistance Committee (DAC), becoming the first former recipient country to become a donor
November 2010	South Korea hosts the 4th G20 summit in Seoul
November 2011	South Korea hosts the OECD High-Level Forum on Aid Effectiveness in Busan
March 2012	South Korea hosts the 2nd Nuclear Security Summit
June 2012	Ten nations sign a treaty making the Korea-led Global Green Growth Institute an international organization
October 2012	South Korea wins a seat on the United Nations Security Council for a two-year term (2013-2015). The Board of the Green Climate Fund votes to locate its permanent headquarters in Songdo, South Korea

Source: Ikenberry.[10]

Careful Considerations

One may be tempted to argue that South Korea's current stance on Russia's invasion of Ukraine can be explained by its desire to uphold and further its middle power status alone. However, the fact remains that Seoul is consistently driven by two critical factors: its long-standing conflict with North Korea and its crucial military alliance with the USA.

The Korean Peninsula (comprising both North and South Korea) has historically suffered because of great-power politics. The two Koreas went to war over Cold War differences in the early 1950s, and the ramifications of that conflict reflect to this day in the divided peninsula. Towards the end of the Korean War, on 1 October 1953, a mutual defence treaty was signed between the USA and South Korea, which guarantees security and stability to the latter. This alliance deters conflict in the region and has provided South Korea with strength and investment, enabling export-led liberalization and an open economy.[11] From being one of the world's poorest countries in the 1950s, South Korea's economic growth leading to an invitation to the G7 has been remarkable.

South Korea's geography necessitates it to maintain its strategic alliance with the USA and compels it to deepen it further. China's rise in the region, Beijing's close partnership with North Korea and Seoul's export market dependence on China are factored into South Korea's decision to continue close relations with the USA.

> 'The primary and enduring tension in South Korean foreign policy and the pursuit of its primary strategic goals of security, prosperity, and national unification is the classic dilemma facing small states surrounded by major powers: the desire for autonomy versus the necessity of alliance with a more powerful security guarantor. South Korea's desire for autonomy versus the necessity of the alliance with the United States has been a source of tension underlying almost every foreign-policy decision made since the country's establishment following World War II. This tension is a natural by-product of South Korea's uniquely situated geography. It exists both as a pivotal partner and a vulnerable neighbour located on the periphery and yet central to larger neighbours' security interests.'[12]

A longer-term consideration for South Korea remains the impact that Russia's invasion of Ukraine might have on North Korea's designs in the Korean Peninsula. Since the war began, North Korea has been one of the handful of countries that supported Russia by opposing a United Nations General Assembly Resolution condemning Russia's invasion. At the same time, it categorically blamed the USA for being the 'root cause of the Ukraine crisis.'[13] Russia's attempts to erase an international border might set a precedent for North Korea, which harbours revisionist plans toward its southern neighbour. The immediate impact of Russia's actions has also encouraged North Korea to continue testing missiles in the region.

Many argue that Russia would not have invaded Ukraine if Kyiv had access to nuclear weapons or if it had successfully joined the North Atlantic Treaty Organization (NATO).

Despite Ukraine's requests for full-scale military assistance, such as troops from the USA or NATO, the West has focused on putting harsh economic penalties on Russia while merely delivering arms to Ukraine. This strategy was mainly designed to avoid a direct military battle resulting in World War III between nuclear-armed states.

Despite being a political and ideological supporter of Russia, China has refused to provide direct military assistance to avoid a direct military conflict with the West. North Korea may realize that it cannot rely on Beijing's military help in the case of an attack by the USA and South Korea, given China's reluctance to actively provide political and military support to Russia during the war in Ukraine. The 1961 Sino-North Korean Friendship Treaty, which includes a collective defence commitment to support one another if either country is under armed attack by a state or alliance of states, was renewed in 2021. Pyongyang may still be concerned that Beijing would be ambivalent in the event of a war on the Korean Peninsula. As the pact can be dissolved any time, North Korea is unlikely to trust China's commitment fully. Furthermore, it is uncertain how Beijing would react if Pyongyang launched an attack on others first, such as Moscow's invasion of Kyiv.[14]

In such a scenario, the Ukraine war has likely reinforced North Korea's idea that it needs to develop its nuclear arsenal to protect the country because support from China is unreliable. Seoul's decisions regarding further deployment of the US military on its territory are deeply marked by the perception of the North Korean threat.

The security dimensions of the Korean Peninsula are going through rapid developments, especially considering the arrival of a new Conservative government in South Korea.

Elected during a global crisis

South Korean President Yoon Suk-yeol assumed office on 10 May 2022. In a pre-election Presidential debate on 25 February, the issue of the Russia-Ukraine conflict was discussed by the two candidates. Yoon advocated stronger trilateral relations with Japan and the USA, including possibly developing an integrated missile defence system among the three countries to counter missile threats from North Korea and China.[15]

The previous Moon Jae-in administration, which had to face the immediate responsibility of responding to the crisis in Ukraine, supported international sanctions on Ukraine. But it was also criticized because of the non-imposition of independent sanctions, like what Australia and Japan did. Despite the criticism, the Moon administration's efforts were explicitly recognized by Secretary of State Anthony Blinken and President Joe Biden of the USA.[16]

In an introductory article in *Foreign Affairs*,[17] President Yoon outlined his foreign policy plans for South Korea and addressed how his government planned to deal with the crisis in Ukraine. The conflict allows Seoul to portray what a 'principled' foreign policy entails—one that works towards 'advancing freedom, peace and prosperity' in defence of a liberal international order. At the United Nations, South Korea voted to condemn Russia's invasion of Ukraine. It later voted to suspend Russia's membership in the United Nations Human Rights Council. South Korea also recently upped its pledge for humanitarian assistance to $40 million.[18]

The crisis provided more cause for the Yoon government to strengthen South Korean defence and deterrence, which was one of his campaign promises. North Korea has even more motive to hold on to nuclear weapons in the wake of the Ukraine crisis. Provocations from North Korea are likely to continue this year, putting negotiations with Pyongyang in jeopardy. The Yoon government now has a more robust political and diplomatic cover to bolster its defence posture and deterrence capabilities due to heightened awareness of security dangers prompted by Russia's incursion.[19]

Conclusion

With the Russian aggression in Ukraine showing no signs of abating, it remains to be seen what steps will be taken by the international community to contain the after-effects of this war.

How Seoul reacts to this crisis will show its commitment to liberal internationalism, its self-perception as a responsible middle power, and its ability to balance the North Korean threat while committing to its biggest alliance partner, the USA.

Under South Korea's desire to be seen as a responsible global actor, Seoul can open the country's borders to allow more refugees to flee the war in Ukraine. This can also offset criticism of strict immigration laws in South Korea and allegations of racism.[20]

Pursuing a more aggressive foreign policy that takes stronger security stances does not come without drawbacks. South Korean export controls and sanctions against Russia and deepened ties with NATO will carry some economic and diplomatic costs for the Yoon government. Russia has already placed South Korea on a list of 'unfriendly countries' released in March 2022.[21] Seoul also has to balance its relationship with China, which is tacitly supporting Russia in its actions. South Korea had suffered economic consequences in the past when Beijing was unhappy with Seoul's overly close military collaboration with Washington during the Terminal High Altitude Area Defence (THAAD) missile system deployment incident. Having that repeated would be detrimental to the country's interests.[22]

Even though the war in Ukraine may seem distant to the South Korean public, the Yoon government has a unique opportunity to leverage this crisis to polish South Korean foreign policy. This provides ample space for reaching out to like-minded countries committed to democratic ideals and international norms. It generates reputational advantages for Seoul by taking on a more significant leadership role in the global sphere and better withstand economic coercion (from China or any other power) in the future. This is South Korea's long-awaited middle power moment.

ENDNOTES

1. 'In Rare Stand, South Korea, Singapore Unveil Sanctions on Russia' *Al Jazeera*, February 28, 2022, https://www.aljazeera.com/economy/2022/2/28/in-rare-stand-south-korea-singapore-unveil-sanctions-on-russia?utm_source=pocket_mylist
2. Society for Worldwide Interbank Financial Telecommunication - provides services related to the execution of financial transactions and payments between banks worldwide.
3. 'Korean Government's Decision Regarding Situation in Ukraine' Ministry of Foreign Affairs, Republic of Korea, 2022, https://www.mofa.go.kr/eng/brd/m_5676/view.do?seq=322003&%3BsrchFr=&%3Bamp%3BsrchTo=&%3Bam3Bamp%3BsrchWord=&%3Bamp%3BsrchTp=&%3Bamp%3Bmulti_itm_se q=0&%3Bamp%3Bitm_seq_1=0&%3Bamp%3Bitm_seq_2=0&%3Bamp%3Bcompany_cd=&%3Bamp%3Bcompany_nm=
4. Scott Snyder, 'Russia's Invasion of Ukraine and Implications for the Korean

Peninsula', Council on Foreign Relations, March 8, 2022, https://www.cfr.org/blog/russias-invasion-ukraine-and-implications-korean-peninsula?utm_source=pocket_mylist
5. Ibid.
6. Jongryn Mo, 'South Korea's Middle Power Diplomacy: A Case of Growing Compatibility between Regional and Global Roles' *International Journal: Canada's Journal of Global Policy Analysis*, 71, no. 4 (2016), pp. 587–607: https://doi.org/10.1177/0020702016686380
7. Ibid., p. 588.
8. Scott Snyder.
9. Zděnek Kríž, Jana Urbanovská, and Stanislava Brajerčíková, 'The Middle Power Concept: Presenting a Complex Approach', *Politické vedy* 22, no. 4 (2019), pp. 33–56: https://doi.org/10.24040/politickevedy.2019.22.4.33-56
10. John Ikenberry, *Rise of Korean Leadership: Emerging Powers and Liberal International Order*, NYC, New York: Palgrave Macmillan, 2015.
11. Scott Snyder, 'South Korea's Strategic Choices' Essay, In *South Korea at the Crossroads: Autonomy and Alliance in an Era of Rival Powers*, pp. 1–19. NYC, New York: Columbia University Press, 2020.
12. Ibid., p. 6.
13. Hyonhee Shin. 'North Korea Blames Ukraine Crisis on 'Hegemonic High-Handedness' of U.S.' Reuters. Thomson Reuters, February 28, 2022. https://www.reuters.com/business/aerospace-defense/north-korea-blames-ukraine-crisis-hegemonic-high-handedness-us-2022-02-28/
14. Sangsoo Lee and Carlotta Bischke, 'What North Korea Thinks about the Russia-Ukraine War', 38 North, May 10, 2022, https://www.38north.org/2022/05/what-north-korea-thinks-about-the-russia-ukraine-war/
15. Scott Snyder, 'A 'Political Novice' Will Soon Be in Charge of South Korean Foreign Policy', Council on Foreign Relations, 2022, https://www.cfr.org/blog/political-novice-will-soon-be-charge-south-korean-foreign-policy.
16. Andrew Yeo, 'How Will South Korea's New President Approach Russia's Ukraine Invasion?' Brookings, May 9, 2022, https://www.brookings.edu/blog/order-from-chaos/2022/05/09/how-will-south-koreas-new-president-approach-russias-ukraine-invasion/
17. Suk-yeol Yoon, 'South Korea Needs to Step Up', *Foreign Affairs*, April 7, 2022, https://www.foreignaffairs.com/articles/south-korea/2022-02-08/south-korea-needs-step
18. Andrew Yeo.
19. Ibid.
20. Erin Aeran Chung, 'How South Korean Demographics Are Affecting Immigration and Social Change - Demographics and the Future of South Korea', Carnegie Endowment for International Peace, June 29, 2021, https://carnegieendowment.org/2021/06/29/how-south-korean-demographics-are-affecting-immigration-and-social-change-pub-84819
21. 'These Are the Countries Russia Considers "Unfriendly"', *Al Jazeera*, March 8, 2022, https://www.aljazeera.com/news/2022/3/8/russia-deals-with-unfriendly-countries-require-moscow-approval
22. Ankit Panda, 'China and South Korea: Examining the Resolution of the THAAD Impasse', *The Diplomat*, November 13, 2017, https://thediplomat.com/2017/11/china-and-south-korea-examining-the-resolution-of-the-thaad-impasse/.

CHAPTER 5

Denuclearisation of North Korea after the Ukraine War: An Uphill Task

Ashu Maan

ABSTRACT

Russia invaded Ukraine on 24 February 2022, citing it as a special military operation.[1] *During the build-up to the war, discussion was repeatedly held on what would have happened if Ukraine had not given up its nuclear weapons in 1992.*[2] *Would Russia have invaded if Ukraine was a nuclear state? Even though several kilometres from the Korean peninsula, the war in Ukraine will have consequences on the denuclearisation of the Democratic People's Republic of Korea (DPRK).*

The DPRK has often cited the fall of Saddam Hussein and Mu'ammar Al-Qadhdhafi as a reason for its pursuance of nuclear weapons. The Ukraine war will embolden the DPRK's claims on nuclear weapons and its defiance of denuclearisation. Relying on archival evidence, this chapter marks the DPRK's nuclear journey and the underlying reasons. It discusses the roles of the Union of Soviet Socialist Republics (Soviet Union) and the People's Republic of China (PRC) in DPRK's nuclearisation journey. The chapter concludes with the problematic prospects of denuclearising the DPRK in the wake of the war.

Key words: *Denuclearisation, Treaty on the Non-Proliferation of Nuclear weapons, DPRK, IAEA, Six Party Talks.*

Introduction

The denuclearisation of the DPRK has been a burning issue since the

Cold War. The United States of America (USA) has come close to war twice with the DPRK over the issue of denuclearisation in 1994[3] and 2002.[4] There have been agreements like the Agreed Framework 1994, the contract on denuclearisation between the DPRK and the Republic of Korea (ROK) of 1994, the Six-Party Talks (involving the DPRK, ROK, PRC, USA, Russia, and Japan), and the Singapore Summit of 2018, to name a few. All these agreements were focused on the denuclearisation of the DPRK, but they failed as soon as they were made due to different expectations of both sides.

While the USA has always used negotiations to demand complete denuclearisation, the DPRK has used them to ask for lifting sanctions and normalising relations. Due to these unreal expectations from both sides, they have often failed to reach a middle ground during the talks and have violated any agreement signed.[5] The last talks regarding denuclearisation were the failed ones between the USA and the DPRK at the Hanoi summit in 2019. Since then, denuclearisation has taken a back seat partly due to the COVID pandemic. However, the issue has again up come into the limelight amid the war in Ukraine.

This chapter first maps the DPRK's journey toward nuclearisation and then discusses why the DPRK wanted the bomb. Further, it discusses the scope of denuclearisation after the Ukraine war and the roles of Russia and the PRC. It is crucial to discuss denuclearisation because, like the DPRK, Ukraine possessed nuclear weapons but let go of them in exchange for security guarantees by the USA, Russia, and the United Kingdom.

To understand the current spate of nuclear tests from the DPRK amidst the unfurling crisis in Ukraine, it becomes pertinent to know how it acquired its atomic arsenals. The DPRK became a de facto nuclear state in 2017 after detonating a nuclear device with a more than 100-kiloton yield.[6] Although the DPRK successfully conducted a nuclear test in 2017, its journey to building a bomb started in the 1950s. DPRK leader Kim Il Jong (1997-2011) wanted to make a nuclear deterrent for the survival of his regime and did everything to acquire a bomb, including asking the PRC for tactical warheads. The DPRK's journey to becoming a nuclear weapons state can be broadly divided into four parts:

1955-1992: Seeking Partnerships

Soon after its formation, the DPRK started seeking nuclear weapons. From 1955 to 1992 it tried to get nuclear technology and equipment from its communist partners, especially the Union of Soviet Socialist Republics (Soviet Union) and the PRC. However, the Soviet Union and the PRC did not want a nuclear-armed DPRK and regularly refused to help or dragged their feet on collaboration.

The DPRK started its journey of acquiring nuclear weapons in 1955 when North Korean Academy of Sciences members attended a nuclear energy conference in Moscow. At the meeting, the DPRK asked for the Soviet Union's assistance in atomic energy, which led to the DPRK and the Soviet Union signing an agreement on nuclear research in 1959. After the deal, the Soviet Union helped the DPRK set up a nuclear research centre, famously called 'The Furniture Factory'.[7] The facility was located on the banks of the Kuryong River, 8 kilometres from the town of Yongbyon.[8]

In 1963, at the PRC's request, the DPRK started looking for information regarding nuclear technology in German Democratic Republic (GDR) universities and research institutes. The DPRK took these actions due to the Sino-Soviet discord and the Soviet Union's move towards non-proliferation by signing a limited Nuclear Test Ban Treaty (NTBT) with the USA and Britain.[9]

On 27 September 1963, the Soviet Ambassador to the DPRK, Vasily Moskovsky, argued against keeping Soviet nuclear specialists in the DPRK due to his fears that it was sending mined ore to the PRC. Vasily also concluded that the Korean side was aggressively trying to extort information from Soviet scientists about the deposits and quality of uranium ore in the Soviet Union.[10] Having been rebuffed by the Soviet Union, the DPRK tried its hand in the PRC. It sent a delegation to the PRC after the PRC detonated its first nuclear device in October 1964. However, like the Soviet Union, Mao refused to help the Koreans and sent them back empty-handed. Finally, relenting in 1965, the Soviet Union sold the DPRK a small four-megawatt research reactor built in the vicinity of Yongbyon.

DPRK leader Kim Il Sung made a secret trip to Moscow in late 1966. He followed it up with a high-level delegation visit to the Soviet Union from 13 February to 3 March 1967. The delegation consisted of Ri Jong-ok (Central Committee member and Chairman of Technical Development), O Jin-U (Deputy Minister of Defence), and O Dinguk (Central Committee member and Chairman of the Commission of Technical Development). Both the visits were aimed to acquire a nuclear power plant from the Soviets. However, the Soviets, unhappy with the progress made at the Yongbyon research reactor, rejected the request by the DPRK. Another reason for the rejection by the Soviet leadership was that DPRK refused to share any data about the reactor's operations with their Soviet counterparts.[11]

Disappointed by the Soviet Union's refusal, the DPRK started looking for other pastures. In December 1967, a delegation of DPRK nuclear experts led by the Vice-Chairman of the Atomic Commission visited the GDR to persuade them to share nuclear technology. During the visit, the DPRK delegation visited mines, industrial plants, and research institutes of atomic sciences. The DPRK delegation put the following demands to the (GDR):

- To sign an agreement on nuclear research.
- Provide equipment necessary for constructing nuclear power plants and share knowledge on the operation of nuclear reactors.
- Exchange of nuclear scientists.

The GDR replied that they were ready to cooperate with the DPRK, but there were some stipulations. The GDR asked the DPRK to make the proposals at the governmental level and include their demands in the scientific and technical cooperation agreement. However, the most significant obstacle in the way of the Koreans was the GDR's insistence on cooperating only if the Soviet Union agreed with it. The DPRK went to the GDR to bypass the Soviet Union, but the GDR insisted on Soviet approval.[12]

The DPRK's nuclear ambitions were hit in 1968 when the Nuclear Non-Proliferation Treaty drafted by the Soviet Union and the USA was submitted to all United Nations (UN) members for signature. The Soviet Union already excluded the DPRK and Romania from providing them with any nuclear technology. The DPRK saw a potential partner in Romania to pressure the Soviet Union to provide them with nuclear technology, but that too was jolted when Romania signed the Treaty on the Non-Proliferation of Nuclear Weapons (NPT) and agreed to International Atomic Energy Agency (IAEA) safeguards. On the other hand, the DPRK refused to sign the Treaty.

The DPRK realised that even emerging nations were capable of developing nuclear weapons by gathering materials and technology from different sources. Its nuclear ambitions were further encouraged by India's 'peaceful' nuclear explosion in 1974. India used a Canadian reactor with heavy water from the USA in its nuclear test. India, like Israel, also became a de facto nuclear-weapon state. The DPRK took note of that and wanted to follow suit but still lacked the technological know-how.

Kim Il Sung at that time had a singular goal, i.e., to reunify Korea and he saw nuclear weapons as a means to that end. With India too acquiring atomic capability, Kim again tried his hand and, this time, instead of asking for nuclear technology, he straightaway asked the PRC for tactical nuclear weapons in 1975. The Hungarian ambassador in Pyongyang sent a report to the Hungarian Foreign Ministry in this regard. He stated that the DPRK had asked the PRC for tactical nuclear weapons 'to offset the nuclear forces in ROK'.[13]

Despite being rebuffed repeatedly by the PRC and the Soviet Union, Kim persevered in his quest for nuclear weapons and sent a DPRK delegation to Moscow in January 1976 to demand that the Soviet Union build a nuclear power plant for the DPRK. The Soviets again refused, citing military considerations and lack of investment.[14] Refusing to budge, the DPRK Deputy Premier Kang Chin-t' ae again asked the Soviet side for a nuclear power plant on the sidelines of the 13th Intergovernmental Consultative Committee held in Moscow from 8 to 11 June 1976.

The Soviets again refused, citing other commitments under the new Five-Year Plan (1976-80).[15] The DPRK again tried to bypass the Soviet Union in acquiring nuclear technology and equipment in 1979 by talking to Czechoslovakia. In February 1979, a DPRK official asked Czechoslovakia to sell uranium-mining equipment and construct a 440-megawatt nuclear power plant in the DPRK. It then had two quarries with uranium content of the core at 0.26 per cent and 0.086 per cent, but significantly lacked mining equipment.[16]

Turned down repeatedly by the Soviet Union, the PRC, and Eastern Europe, the DPRK decided to go solo in its quest to build nuclear weapons in the early 1980s. (See Annexure 1) It started work on a thirty-megawatt research reactor near the site of the research reactor set up by the Soviet Union in 1959. The build-up was spotted by a US satellite in 1982.[17] Unlike the Soviet-built 'water-water energy reactor' (VVER) in Eastern Europe, the DPRK built a gas graphite-moderated (Reaktorbolshoymoshchnostykanalny) RBMK reactor that operated on natural uranium fuel.[18]

VVER reactors needed enriched uranium and creating a bomb from it was challenging. However, the RBMK reactors used natural uranium as fuel, which, when irradiated, worked as an ideal source of weapons-grade plutonium. The resulting plutonium was enough to build at least five nuclear warheads.[19]

Despite little to no help from the Soviet Union, the DPRK indigenous nuclear program was developing rapidly. The USA took note of it and urged the Soviet Union to try to persuade the DPRK again to sign the NPT. If it signed the NPT, the Soviet Union agreed to provide the DPRK with power reactors. However, despite signing the NPT, the DPRK had still not reached a safeguards agreement with the IAEA.

In 1991, the IAEA board called upon the DPRK to implement a safeguards agreement. In turn, the DPRK asked for security assurances from the USA that included it withdrawing nuclear weapons from the ROK. In reply, the USA announced the withdrawal of tactical nuclear weapons from foreign bases[20] to decrease its global atomic footprint. As a result of the US initiative, the DPRK agreed to IAEA safeguards and signed an agreement with the ROK not to develop a nuclear weapon.

The North Korean Nuclear Crisis (February 1992-May 1994) and NPT

The initial peace with the DPRK agreeing to IAEA safeguards was short-lived. The DPRK refused to ratify the IAEA safeguards. Further, US intelligence concluded that the DPRK was nearing the capacity to develop nuclear weapons. This was when the PRC and Russia were looking to improve their relations with the USA and therefore pressurised the DPRK to ratify the safeguards agreement. Although the DPRK confirmed the safeguards agreement in 1992, suspicions remained. IAEA inspectors found evidence of equipment removed from the reprocessing plant that the DPRK had previously denied.

Further, the DPRK impeded access to undeclared sites allegedly storing nuclear waste. The IAEA also concluded that the DPRK had produced weapons-grade plutonium.[21] This led to more pressure on it from the USA, Russia, Europe, and the PRC to comply with IAEA safeguards fully. In March 1993, the USA and the ROK restarted their military exercises that had been halted after the DPRK signed the NPT.

The USA aimed the move to pressure the DPRK to allow IAEA special inspections of its alleged nuclear waste sites. However, the tactic turned on its head, leading to the DPRK declaring that it would withdraw from the NPT in 90 days. The USA doubled down and took the issue to the UNSC. However, after seeing signals by the PRC that it would not support sanctions against the DPRK, the USA backed down and again resorted to diplomacy.[22]

After engaging diplomatically with the DPRK, the USA got an assurance from it to suspend its NPT withdrawal in exchange for helping them acquire light-power reactors. The DPRK probably saw the PRC's reluctance to support sanctions against it as a bulwark against the USA. The USA agreed to help the DPRK acquire light power reactors when it threatened to quit the NPT. The DPRK saw it as an opportunity to extort more from the USA and again started dragging its feet on inspections.

This was also when US intelligence concluded that the DPRK may already have acquired enough plutonium to build a nuclear device. The DPRK's actions bore fruit, and the USA and the ROK agreed to suspend their joint military exercises in exchange for the DPRK agreeing to new IAEA inspections in March 1994[23].

After getting concessions, the DPRK again pulled a fast one and blocked IAEA inspectors from visiting its reprocessing plants. Having had enough, the USA restarted military exercises with the ROK and moved Patriot missile batteries there.[24] The PRC again acted as a deterrent in punishing the DPRK (by opposing sanctions) due to which the USA again backed down.

Meanwhile, the IAEA concluded that it had lost the ability to verify if the DPRK had diverted nuclear materials for use to a weapons program. Tensions rose and probably were this high for the first time since 1950. The severity of the situation can be best described by President Clinton's special envoy William Perry's discussion with ROK President Kim Dae

Jung. William Perry said during the debate that 'the United States had planned for war in 1994, and with 'the combined forces of ROK and United States, we can undoubtedly win this war'.[25]

The Framework Agreement and NPT (1994-2003)

The USA, aware of the fallout of another Korean war, again tried its hand at diplomacy and sent former President Jimmy Carter to negotiate with Kim Il Sung in June 1994. President Carter started a mutual framework negotiation with Kim Il Sung that was finished by his son, Kim Jong Il, after Il Sung died amid the talks in July 1994. The framework agreement led the DPRK to discontinue operations at its nuclear sites in Yongbyon, new inspections by IAEA, remain in the NPT and implement the 1992 denuclearisation pact with the ROK. In return, the USA agreed to provide the DPRK with heavy oil, acquire two light-water power reactors, remove sanctions, and increase diplomatic contacts.[26]

Like the previous agreements and understandings, this agreement, too, ran into difficulties. However, this time it was not due to the DPRK entirely. The USA was regularly late in providing oil to the DPRK. Like the Soviet Union in 1985, it was dragging its feet on the light-water reactors. The USA still kept the DPRK on the list of state sponsors of terror, and there were little to no indications of normalising relations.

The DPRK was going through economic turmoil in 1997. Meanwhile, it carried on with its work of building a bomb. United States intelligence in 1998 'detected the construction of a large underground complex in the DPRK' that they worried was a covert nuclear site. Further, United States intelligence concluded in the same year that the DPRK was procuring components that could be used for an enrichment program.

Interestingly, this time, the DPRK did not try to procure equipment from its traditional partners, i.e., the PRC and Russia; instead, it banked on Pakistan or, more specifically, the A.Q. Khan network.[27] Pakistan, through A.Q. Khan, provided the DPRK with a centrifuge, and in return, Pakistan received the Dudong missile from the DPRK.[28] Despite the DPRK's misgivings, the USA still followed a policy of engagement with it.

The US State Department assessed that a 'starving North Korea' can lead to instability and create a 'dangerously chaotic situation'.[29] Its assessment led to another round of talks between the USA and the DPRK in 1999. This time, the DPRK agreed to halt its missile tests, and the USA, in turn, agreed to ease economic sanctions.

The next hurdle in the DPRK's denuclearisation came after the 9/11 attacks on New York. The USA under President Bush accused it of enriching uranium secretly and added it to the 'axis of evil'. The US actions led to the breakdown of the Framework Agreement. Further, the DPRK withdrew from the NPT, expelled the IAEA inspectors, and restarted its nuclear activities at Yongbyon.[30] The USA in turn cut off oil shipments to the DPRK and halted work on the light water reactors it had promised earlier.

Testing the Bomb: Successful Nuclearization of the DPRK

Learning from dealing with the USA in the past, the DPRK tried to extort concessions by threatening to conduct a nuclear test and export atomic devices. Its actions led the USA to start multilateral negotiations with the DPRK. The negotiations were called six-party talks that included the USA, the PRC, Russia, Japan, the ROK, and the DPRK. Despite the talks, the DPRK continued its nuclear activities as US intelligence in 2005 detected a tunnel in the DPRK that could be used for conducting a nuclear test. The DPRK was still participating in the Six-Party Talks and, in September 2005, agreed to denuclearisation.[31]

The USA, in an attempt to push the DPRK into a corner, imposed new sanctions on DPRK officials and promised further economic sanctions. The US strategy again backfired as the DPRK halted the Six-Party Talks and tested six missiles.[32] The missile tests led to additional sanctions from the UNSC. In the wake of the sanctions, the DPRK threatened a nuclear test and this time conducted one. The test is reported to have been a relative failure with less than one-kiloton yield.[33] The UNSC imposed further sanctions on the DPRK covering trade in luxury goods. However, the PRC and Russia's opposition weakened the proper implementation of the sanctions.

If the DPRK continued its actions, the PRC had a lot to lose, so it compelled the DPRK to re-engage in the Six-Party Talks. After the talks resumed, the involved parties reached an agreement in 2007 that called for the DPRK to halt its plutonium program and accept IAEA inspections at the Yongbyon facility. In exchange, the USA was to lift economic sanctions on the DPRK and take it off its list of state sponsors of terrorism.[34]

This is another example of the DPRK's strategy to extort concessions from the USA. It would threaten the USA and the ROK with missile or nuclear tests. Then, after the USA indicated sanctions, the DPRK would bank on the PRC to veto them to bring the USA to the negotiating table. After the USA came to negotiate, the DPRK would ask for economic concessions. The 2007 agreement, like many before it, was doomed to fail from the start, mainly because of deep distrust between the USA and the DPRK.

While the USA came through on some of its promises in the 2007 agreements, it refused to remove the DPRK from its list of state sponsors of terrorism.[35] The situation flared up again when the DPRK conducted a missile test of the Taepdong-2 missile in April 2009, leading to more sanctions by the UNSC. The DPRK responded to the sanctions by expelling the IAEA inspectors, pulling out of the Six-Party Talks and publicly threatening to resume its nuclear program. It upped its antics in 2010 by sinking a ROK ship shelling the island of Yeonpyeong.

The USA, under the Obama Administration, adopted a policy of 'wait and watch', while it decided to apply economic and political pressure on the DPRK through the UNSC and the PRC. The DPRK agreed to temporarily limit its nuclear and missile activities in exchange for relaxed sanctions in 2012. However, like all the previous agreements, it violated it pretty quickly. After this point, it refused negotiations with the USA until 2017. The period between 2010 and 2017 was when the DPRK conducted most nuclear and missile tests. It conducted one nuclear test in 2013, two trials in 2016, and one test in 2017. The last test in September 2017 was estimated to exceed 100 kilotons in yield. This was a massive leap from a yield of less than one kiloton in 2006 to more than 100 kilotons in 2017. With the 2017 test, it became a de facto nuclear power.

Denuclearisation of the DPRK

The war in Ukraine has raised one pertinent question in everyone's mind observing the DPRK. Considering what happened to Ukraine, will it be possible to make the DPRK denuclearise? After the disintegration of the Soviet Union, Ukraine inherited nuclear weapons that were a part of the Soviet arsenal. Albeit Ukraine never had operational control over the weapons, it decided to transfer them to Russia and, along with Belarus and Kazakhstan, joined the Lisbon Protocol[36] in 1991.

Furthermore, Ukraine got security assurances[37] from Russia, the USA, and the United Kingdom regarding its sovereignty after signing the NPT in 1994. However, those security assurances were insufficient since one of the signatories, i.e., Russia, violated Ukraine's territorial sovereignty twice in the last decade. The DPRK sees nuclear weapons as a necessary deterrent against an invasion by the USA. Will it be willing to give up its nuclear weapons in place of the same security guarantees that Ukraine received? To answer this question, we need to first look at why the DPRK built the bomb.

Why the Bomb?

The DPRK's decision to build the bomb defies many proliferation theories. The Neorealist theory by Kenneth Waltz states that the international system is anarchical, and states have to rely on self-help to protect their sovereignty. In their own words, the DPRK built the bomb because 'The DPRK made nuclear weapons and has strengthened its self-defensive war deterrent to maintain the sovereignty and the right to existence of the nation in the face of the increasingly aggressive threat by the United States'.[38] The DPRK signed the Treaty of Mutual Friends with the Soviet Union[39] and the PRC[40] in 1961. It signed them as a bulwark against the American threat. With the signing of the treaties, the DPRK came under the Soviet Union's nuclear umbrella and later the PRC's after 1964. Still, it pursued atomic weapons.

According to Scott D. Sagan's security model of nuclear proliferation, 'Because of the enormous destructive power of nuclear weapons, any state that seeks to maintain its national security must balance against any rival state that develops nuclear weapons by gaining access to a nuclear deterrent itself.' Regime security has been paramount to DPRK since its inception. The DPRK was in an existential competition with the ROK. The Mutual Defence Treaty with the USA strengthened the ROK's military, which placed US troops and nuclear weapons on its soil.

The DPRK, too had a defence treaty with the Soviet Union and the PRC. However, neither of them placed troops or nuclear weapons on Korean soil. The DPRK had significantly less trust in the Soviet Union for two reasons. First, it did not give diplomatic backing to the DPRK when the USA threatened to use nuclear weapons during the Korean war. The second was the August Faction incident,[41] when the Soviet Union and the PRC tried to enforce a coup in the DPRK.

The DPRK's security environment further deteriorated in the early 1990s after the disintegration of the Soviet Union. The end of the Soviet Union also brought about an end to the financial assistance from the Soviet bloc. This was also when the PRC actively engaged with the West, focusing on its economic development. In its bid for economic rise, the PRC recognised the ROK and established economic relations with it.

These changes were too much for the DPRK. Other geopolitical events did not help the DPRK's situation. In October 2002, its Vice Minister of Foreign Affairs, Kang Sok-Ju, told his American counterpart, 'We are a part of the axis of evil...if we disarm ourselves because of US pressure, we will become like Yugoslavia or Afghanistan's Taliban, to be beaten to death'.[42] The Korean minister's statement more than sums up the argument of why getting the bomb was of utmost importance for Korea.

Denuclearisation after the War

The war in Ukraine, after it ends, will have done nothing but strengthen the DPRK's resolve against denuclearisation. The DPRK agreed to complete denuclearisation at the Singapore Summit in 2018.[43] However, like the previous agreements, it did not substantiate, and it continues proliferation. The question one needs to ask now is whether the complete denuclearisation of the DPRK is possible. It already saw nuclear weapons as necessary for survival and was against denuclearisation. This was evident in 2006 when American nuclear scientist Seigfried Hecker visited the DPRK. Its officials told Hecker that 'their negotiation strategy had changed. They considered DPRK a nuclear power and wanted to talk arms control with Washington; not denuclearisation focused on the North'.[44]

The war in Ukraine has further emboldened the DPRK's claims to nuclear weapons as a necessity for its survival. According to estimates by US intelligence, the DPRK had 20-30 nuclear weapons and fissile material for another 65 weapons.[45] A report by RAND Corporation in 2021 projected that the DPRK could have around two hundred nuclear weapons and hundreds of ballistic missiles stockpiled by 2027.[46] In such a situation, the immediate goal of the USA should not be denuclearisation but non-proliferation.[47]

Rather than coerce the DPRK to denuclearise, the USA should look to negotiate with the DPRK on their security concerns, energy, and the economy. Both the countries should look to return to an arrangement like the Framework Agreement of 1994. The essential thing should be to halt nuclear tests and missile launches. In return, the USA should offer to gradually lift economic sanctions according to the DPRK's behaviour. It is also necessary to get it to halt the production of fissile material and then diplomatically work towards rolling back the nuclear weapons program and eliminating it.

Role of PRC and Russia

After the Cold War, the world is again in a Great Power rivalry between the PRC and the USA. The rivalry raises the question if the denuclearisation of the DPRK will become a point of contention or collaboration between the PRC and the USA. Before Russia invaded Ukraine, the PRC and Russia released a joint statement.[48] The statement characterised the Russia-PRC relationship as a close and comprehensive strategic partnership or, in Putin's words, 'a relationship that probably cannot be compared with anything in the world.'

Going by the joint statement, it is safe to assume that going forward, the Dragonbear[49] (Russia and the PRC) will primarily have a convergence on matters such as the DPRK. Before the normalisation of the relationship, the PRC used the DPRK as a buffer against the USA. The PRC also continuously shielded the DPRK in the UNSC from sanctions. While the PRC had always been against DPRK's nuclear proliferation, it got strict with them only when their behaviour triggered the US military presence in the region.[50]

The PRC's strategy for denuclearisation has passed through two stages. The first was during the first North Korean nuclear crisis in the early 1990s. At that time, the PRC's strategy was to maintain the DPRK's stability and support it in negotiating bilaterally with the USA. The PRC's strategy was informed by its belief that a stable DPRK was vital to its security interests. This was also the reason why the PRC opposed international sanctions on the DPRK.[51] However, after the collapse of the Soviet Union, the PRC became the DPRK's lone patron and joined the multilateral Six-Party Talks. This was when the PRC's economy was increasing due to assistance from the USA. Therefore, the PRC started supporting sanctions against the DPRK but still followed the policy of a stable DPRK.

However, things have changed now as opposed to the early 2000s. The PRC and the USA are in strategic competition with each other. During such competition, the PRC's strategy of using the DPRK as a buffer against the USA may make a comeback. As Samir Saran stated in his book '*Pax Sinica*', the PRC continued its growth under the radar because the USA was busy in Afghanistan, Iraq, and the Middle East. In the PRC, there have been voices that claim that it is in the 'PRC's strategic interests to leave the United States tied up with the nuclear crisis.'

The USA, under the Biden Administration, considers the PRC as its biggest threat; meanwhile, Russia and the DPRK have been identified as secondary threats.[52] In such a situation, it would make strategic sense for the PRC if the USA was distracted and not focused primarily on the PRC. It has indicated this strategy by refusing to support fresh sanctions against the DPRK for its missile tests during the Ukraine war. This marks the PRC's return to the pre-1991 system, which covered the DPRK by refusing to support sanctions by using a veto in the United Nations Security Council.[53]

Russia shares the same thinking regarding denuclearisation. The Russian president has supported the DPRK's nuclear program in the past. While Russia had historically supported denuclearisation, that thinking has been changing. At a press conference after the 2017 BRICS summit,[54] Putin said that the 'DPRK did not have any other choice but to develop weapons of mass destruction in the interest of self-preservation.' Putin also used an analogy for the DPRK's behaviour by referring to what happened to the leaders of Iraq (Saddam Hussein) and Libya (Mummar Gadaffi) when they abandoned their weapons of mass destruction.[55] Russia's current actions in Ukraine and Putin's changing stance on the DPRK indicate that, unlike in the Cold War, Russia may not support denuclearisation.

Considering Russia's new alliance and its probable stand on the DPRK, the USA might have to go it alone in negotiating with the DPRK. In such a situation, step-by-step non-proliferation, easing economic sanctions and then denuclearisation might be the best way for the USA.

ENDNOTES

1. Al Jazeera. "No other option: Excerpts of Putin's speech declaring war", February 24, 2022, https://www.aljazeera.com/news/2022/2/24/putins-speech-declaring-war-on-ukraine-translated-excerpts
2. Broad, William. Ukraine Gave up a Giant Arsenal 30 Years Ago. Today There Are Regrets, February 5, 2022, https://www.nytimes.com/2022/02/05/science/ukraine-nuclear-weapons.html
3. National Security Archives. "Cable, Embassy Seoul 6928 to SecState", December 8, 1998, Subject: Former Secretary Perry's Meeting with President Kim (Confidential), https://nsarchive.gwu.edu/sites/default/files/documents/5750507/National-Security-Archive-Doc-10-Cable-Seoul.pdf
4. Nicholas J. Wheeler. "To Put Oneself into the Other Fellow's Place': John Herz, the Security Dilemma, and the Nuclear Age." *International Relations*, 2008, Vol. 22 (4): pp. 493-509.
5. Moore, Gregory. America's Failed North Korea Nuclear Policy: A New Approach, *Asian Perspective*, 2008, pp. 9-27.
6. BBC. "North Korea: What we know about its missile and nuclear programme", March 24, 2022, https://www.bbc.com/news/world-asia-41174689
7. Narang, Vipin. *Seeking the Bomb: Strategies of Nuclear Proliferation*, Princeton, Princeton University Press, 2022.
8. Ibid.
9. Wilson Centre. "Conversation between Soviet Ambassador in North Korea Vasily Moskovsky and the German Ambassador," August 26, 1963, History and Public Policy Program Digital Archive, AVPRF, obtained and translated for NKIDP by Sergey Radchenko, https://digitalarchive.wilsoncenter.org/document/110608
10. Wilson Centre. "Conversation between Soviet Ambassador in North Korea Vasily Moskovsky and Soviet Specialists in North Korea," September 27, 1963, History and Public Policy Program Digital Archive, AVPRF, fond 0102, opis 19, papka 97, delo 5, listy 161-162. Obtained and translated for NKIDP by Sergey Radchenko. https://digitalarchive.wilsoncenter.org/document/110611
11. Wilson Centre. "Report, Embassy of Hungary in North Korea to the Hungarian Foreign Ministry," March 13, 1967, History and Public Policy Program Digital Archive, MOL, XIX-J-1-j Korea, 1967, 61. doboz, 5, 002126/1967. Obtained and translated for NKIDP by Balazs Szalontai. https://digitalarchive.wilsoncenter.org/document/110621
12. Wilson Centre. "Report, Embassy of Hungary in North Korea to the Hungarian Foreign Ministry," February 29, 1968, History and Public Policy Program Digital Archive, MOL, XIX-J-1-j Korea, 1968, 58. doboz, 5, 001871/1968. Obtained and translated for NKIDP by Balazs Szalontai. https://digitalarchive.wilsoncenter.org/document/110626
13. Wilson Centre. "Report, Embassy of Hungary in North Korea to the Hungarian Foreign Ministry," July 30, 1975, History and Public Policy Program Digital Archive, MOL, XIX-J-1-j Korea, 1975, 83. doboz, 81-10, 002835/8/1975. Obtained and translated for NKIDP by Balazs Szalontai https://digitalarchive.wilsoncenter.org/document/111468
14. "Report, Embassy of Hungary in North Korea to the Hungarian Foreign Ministry," April 15, 1976, History and Public Policy Program Digital Archive, MOL, XIX-J-1-

j Korea, 1976, 82. doboz, 5, 00854/2/1976. Obtained and translated for NKIDP by Balazs Szalontai. https://digitalarchive.wilsoncenter.org/document/111473

15. "Telegram, Embassy of Hungary in North Korea to the Hungarian Foreign Ministry," June 25, 1976, History and Public Policy Program Digital Archive, MOL, XIX-J-1-j Korea, 1976, 82. doboz, 5, 00854/5/1976. Obtained and translated for NKIDP by Balazs Szalontai. https://digitalarchive.wilsoncenter.org/document/111475
16. "Telegram, Embassy of Hungary in North Korea to the Hungarian Foreign Ministry," February 17, 1979, History and Public Policy Program Digital Archive, MOL, XIX-J-1-j Korea, 1979, 81. doboz, 81-5, 001583/1979. Obtained and translated for NKIDP by Balazs Szalontai https://digitalarchive.wilsoncenter.org/document/110133
17. Wampler, Robert A. ed. 2003. *North Korea and Nuclear Weapons: The Declassified U.S. Record. National Security Archive Electronic Briefing Book*, No. 87, at www.gwu.edu/~nsarchiv/NSAEBB/NSAEBB87/#docs (accessed May 13, 2022).
18. Valtonen, K.. "VVER and RMBK reactors", IAEA, Report Number LTKK-TJ—41, at https://inis.iaea.org/search/searchsinglerecord.aspx?recordsFor=SingleRecord&RN=26047594
19. Wit, Joel S., Daniel B. Poneman, and Robert L. Gallucci. 2004. Going Critical: The First North Korean Nuclear Crisis. Washington, DC: Brookings Institution.
20. Rosenbaum, D. E. (1991, October 20). U.S. to pull A-Bombs from South Korea. *The New York Times*. Retrieved May 15, 2022, from https://www.nytimes.com/1991/10/20/world/us-to-pull-a-bombs-from-south-korea-html
21. Richelson, Jeffrey. *Spying on the Bomb*, New York, W. W. Norton & Company, 2007.
22. Reiss, Mitchell. *Bridled Ambition: Why countries constrain their Nuclear capabilities*, Maryland, John Hopkins University Press, 1995.
23. Michaels, J. U. T. (2018, June 12). U.S. will suspend military drills with South Korea, but they can be restarted quickly. *USA Today*. Retrieved May 15, 2022, from https://eu.usatoday.com/story/news/world/2018/06/12/trump-suspend-military-exercises-south-korea/693527002/
24. Reiss, Mitchell. *Bridled Ambition: Why countries constrain their Nuclear capabilities*, Maryland, John Hopkins University Press, 1995.
25. U.S. Department of State. Cable, Embassy Seoul 6928 to SecState, December 8,1998, Subject: Former Secretary Perry's meeting with President Kim (Confidential), https://nsarchive.gwu.edu/sites/default/files/documents/4323441/Document-07-Cable-Amembassy-Seoul-6928-to.pdf
26. International Atomic Energy Agency, "Agreed Framework of 21 October 1994 Between the United States of America and the Democratic People's Republic of Korea," https://www.iaea.org/publications/documents/inficrs/agreed-framework-21-october-1994-between-united-states-america-and-democratic-peoples-republic-korea
27. Pollack, Jonathan. *No Exit: North Korea, Nuclear Weapons, and International Security*, London, Routledge, 2011.
28. DW, Pakistan's indirect role in North Korea's nuclear program, https://www.dw.com/en/pakistans-indirect-role-in-orth-koreas-nuclear-program/a-40507693
29. National Security Archive, State Department Background Paper: North Korea, drafted by John Meakem, East Asia and Pacific Affairs, ca. April 14, 1998 (Secret),

https://nsarchive.gwu.edu/document/16095-document-03-state-department-backgroound-paper
30. Richelson, Jeffrey. *Spying on the Bomb*, New York, W. W. Norton & Company, 2007, pp. 530-532.
31. Hecker, S. S. Lessons Learned from the North Korean Nuclear Crisis, 139(1), pp. 44-56.
32. Sanger, D. E. (2006, October 4), North Koreans say They Plan a Nuclear Test, *The New York Times*, Retrieved May 15, 2022, https://www.nytimes.com/2006/10/04/world/asia/04Korea.html.
33. Lan. H. "North Korea's Nuclear Programme and its Impacts on Regional Security, United Service Institution of India, 2017, https://usiofindia.org/publication/usi-journal/north-koreas-nuclear-programme-and-its-impacts-on-regional-security/
34. U.S. Department of State, "North Korea Denuclearization Action Plan." February 13, 2007, https://2001-2009.state.gov/r/pa/prs/ps/2007/february/80479.htm
35. Arms Control Association, "Chronology of U.S.-North Korean and Missile Diplomacy," January 2018, https://www.armscontrol.org/factsheet/dprkchron
36. Arms Control Association. "The Lisbon Protocol At a Glance", December 2020, https://www.armscontrol.org/nod/3289
37. United Nations, "Memorandum on security assurances in connection with Ukraine's accession to the Treaty on the Non-Proliferation of Nuclear Weapons", Budapest, 5 December 1994, https://treaties.un.org/doc/Publication/UNTS/Volume%203007/Part/volume-3007-I-52241.pdf
38. Hecker, Seigfried, Lessons learned from the North Korean nuclear crises, American Academy of Arts & Sciences, 139 (1), 2010, pp. 44-56.
39. Union of Soviet Socialist Republics and Democratic People's Republic of Korea, Treaty of friendship, co-operation, and mutual assistance, signed at Moscow, July 6, 1961.
40. Peoples' Republic of China and Democratic People's Republic of Korea, Treaty of Friendship, co-operation and mutual assistance, July 11, 1961.
41. Hall, David, The 1956 August Plenum Incident: An Historiographical Analysis, *North Korean Review*, 16 (2), pp. 101-110.
42. Pritchard, Charles. *Failed Diplomacy: The Tragic Story of How North Korea Got the Bomb*, Washington D.C., Brookings Institution Press, 2007, p. 25.
43. Joint Statement of President Donald J. Trump of the United States of America and Chairman Kim Jong Un of the Democratic People's Republic of Korea at the Singapore Summit, June 12, 2018, https://trumpwhitehouse.archives.gov/briefings-statements/joint-statement-president-donald-j-trump-united-states-america-chairman-kim-jong-un-democratic-peoples-republic-korea-singapore-summit/
44. Hecker, Seigfried. Lessons learned from the North Korean nuclear crises, American Academy of Arts & Sciences, 139 (1), 2010, pp. 44-56.
45. Council on Foreign Relations, North Korea's Military Capabilities, 22 December 2021, https://www.cfr.org/background/north-korea-nuclear-weapons-missile-tests-military-capabilities
46. RAND Corporation, Countering the risks of North Korean Nuclear Weapons, 2021.
47. Dealing with Russia and North Korea: An interview with Siegfried Hecker.
48. Joint Statement of the Russian Federation and the People's Republic of China on the International Relations Entering a New Era and the Global Sustainable

Development, February 4, 2022, http://en.kremlin.ru/supplement/5770

49. The term 'Dragonbear' was first used by Velina Tchakarova in the context of the Russia-China alliance.
50. Song, J.Y. (2011). "Understanding China's Response to North Korea's Provocations" The Dual Threats Model." *Asian Survey* 51, pp. 1134-1155.
51. Kim, Patricia. How China Sees North Korea: Three Critical Moments in History and Future Directions, Chicago Council on Global Affairs, 2018.
52. National Interest, Pentagon Completes 2022 National Defense Strategy, March 30, 2022, https://nationalinterest.org/blog/buzz/pentagon-completes-2022-national-defense-strategy-201543
53. Chung, Chaewon. China signals it won't support new sanctions if North Korea tests nuclear weapon, June 2, 2022, https: www.nknews.org/2022/06/china-signals-it-wont-support-sanctions-if-north-korea-tests-nuclear-weapon/
54. 'Vladimir Putin's news conference following BRICS Summit', President of Russia, September 5, 2017, en.kremlin.ru/events/president/news/55535
55. Westermann, Jacqueline. Putin, and North Korea: Exploring Russian interests around the peninsula, Australian Strategic Policy Institute, 2018.

CHAPTER 6

Crisis in Ukraine, Political Brainstorming in Japan: The Curious Case of Tokyo's Response to Putin's Invasion

Ashutosh Kumar

ABSTRACT

Russia's unprovoked military aggression against Ukraine has come as a dire security warning for many states and upended assumptions about the likelihood of a great power war. The war has led to a significant diplomatic rift between Japan and Russia. The land-grabbing game in Eastern Europe has made many states apprehensive about their own strategic outlook and security posture. The sudden war has also changed the geopolitical variables in North-East Asia, making Japan nervous about future Chinese and Russian aggression discourse on similar lines in the Indo-Pacific region. The war has pushed Japan to take some tough policy decisions against Russia. The regime of Japanese Prime Minister Fumio Kishida and the Japanese public has come out with bold reactions against Moscow's unilateral imposition of war on Ukraine. This chapter analyses Japan's response, which three considerations can determine; the resoluteness of Japan to set precedents for certain status quo changing behaviours; second, sanctions on the Russian entity, and; third, domestic de-securitisation of 'Japan's imperialist identity' mobilising public opinion for bolder revisionist debates. This chapter concludes that Tokyo's reaction to the Ukraine war has changed the political narratives in Japan's political sphere and public perception, resulting in the Japanese quest to be a 'Normal State.'

Key Words: *Japan, Russia, Ukraine, War, Response, De-securitisation, Temporal Other.*

Introduction

Putin's recent move of military action in Eastern Europe has made the Japanese political echelon nervous. It has led to the rise of 'Temporal Russia,' where the policies of the Moscow regime are manifested in revisionism and changing the status quo. For long, Japan has been considered a 'pariah' in the international world order. However, in recent years, international relations scholars have questioned Japan's 'Pacifist identity.' The recent invasion of Ukraine and growing geopolitical uncertainty has propelled Tokyo's policymakers to reconsider their strategic and security outlook. The military adventure of Russia has drawn concerns and comparisons to what China may have in mind for Taiwan or the Senkaku islands. In Japan, the public is debating what Ukraine's invasion could mean for the East Asian region, adding a plethora of momentum to Japan's objective of acquiring 'Enemy base strike capability'.

Japanese Prime Minister Fumio Kishida of the LDP (Liberal Democratic Party), who passed his most prominent political test on 31 October 2021,[1] is taking tough diplomatic decisions on the Russian aggression. He is trying to show how Japan stood its ground coming out of its pacifist comfort zone. Putin's unprovoked invasion of Kyiv has come as a direct security warning and implications for many states around the globe. The horrifying socio-economic destruction and civilian casualties in Ukraine have prompted world leaders to rethink their strategic posture and security policies. The war has shaken all the countries of the world. Countries like Finland and Sweden represent the most notable cases of strategic reappraisals and security revivalism after following a grand strategy to ensure smooth and peaceful coexistence with Moscow. However, with the outbreak of war in Eastern Europe, Scandinavian nations following independent security policies are now tilting toward joining NATO.

Japan cannot remain insulated from the seismic shift triggered by the war in Ukraine. The effect of the war on the West has now breached the political nervousness in North-East Asia, and Japan is not left behind in this security dilemma. Acting in cohesion with the United States of America (USA) and European powers, the Tokyo regime has stepped up its sanctions against Russia. Japanese Prime Minister Fumio Kishida's announcements of a barrage of sanctions against Russia following the invasion mark a significant shift in Tokyo's foreign policy rhetoric, bringing it in line with the challenging position of G7 countries.

The mainstream international relations theories have considered Japan a 'status quo power.[2,3] However, in recent years, Japan's international response to changing status quo behaviour has changed dramatically. On 1 March 2022, Japan's lower house adopted a strong resolution condemning Putin's move as 'unacceptable' and a 'serious breach of international order'. The resolution, approved by an overwhelming majority, goes on to underline that Russia's action in Ukraine could shake the foundation of the international order, including the Indo-Pacific. It intends to follow the path of an immobilising global strategy toward revisionist powers like China and Russia.

Status Quoist or Change In Outlook?

Kishida's government surprised many nations with its strong condemnation of Russia's invasion, in contrast to its diplomatic hesitancy to take action against Russia after the 2014 war in Crimea. Looking back to the year 2014, when Russia's President Vladimir Putin annexed Crimea, the Tokyo regime of the then Prime Minister Shinzo Abe refrained from imposing sanctions on Russia thus breaking the chain of sanctions by its Western allies. Tokyo's response to the current Moscow invasion stands in sharp contrast to its 2014 diplomatic reaction when the Abe government imposed symbolic sanctions in response to Russia's annexation of Crimea. At that time, the government muted the public response, feeling that Crimea was a far distant issue that did not affect the Japanese. This time, the Tokyo government has taken a clear and robust posture against Moscow's aggression, hedging with its net security provider, the USA, and Europe in putting pressure on Russia.

Nevertheless, while these diplomatic manoeuvrings reflect shifts in Tokyo's approach to the international world order, its relations with Europe and Russia due to the Ukraine crisis suggest that the current foreign policy trajectory may apply to Japan's future foreign policy discourse. Recently, Japan announced that the nation would accept refugees from the troubled region of Eastern Europe and sent bulletproof vests to Ukraine. These extraordinary measures taken by the Kishida regime point towards a whole new ball game regarding Japan accepting refugees.[5–7] The political decisions were made without any '*gaiatsu*,'*[8,9] or external pressure, underscoring Tokyo's determination to show its will to support Ukraine. This new stance deifies the pacifist identity of Japan. By this, the Tokyo regime established precedents for certain status quo changing behaviours: in this case, Putin's military adventure in Eastern Europe.

Russia's troubling actions in Eastern Europe, the recent attack on the Ukrainian power plant, and the mass killing in Bucha have triggered alarm bells around the globe. The military aggression by Russia has a significant impact on Japan being a 'normal power.' The geopolitical tussle is likely to accelerate Tokyo's debate over its defence and security policy, which has always been a musing point in Japan amid Chinese expansionist aims. The problematic international world order has raised serious questions about Japan's security readiness and geopolitical crisis management capabilities under its war-renouncing** constitution[10]—a long-stagnant and controversial debate—as part of its national security policy. Akihisa Shiozaki, a conservative LDP (Liberal Democratic Party) member, recently opined that "It is a big awakening that there are limitations to what the UN can do, limits to what diplomacy can do, regulations to what economic sanctions can do".[11] Shiozaki pointed out the new shift of policy on refugees as a country bracing for recent political changes. Considering the future apprehensions and crisis scenarios in East Asia, including the Taiwan Strait contingency, Japan is building the capacity to respond to refugees during a world emergency. However, details of Japan's refugee decision are still pending, and it is interesting to see how many refugees the country will accept.

Although Putin's invasion has reconfigured the security and geopolitical landscape in Europe and East Asia, the full impact on the Indo-Pacific region is yet to be seen. Experts are debating whether the military invasion in Ukraine will mark a new turning point for Tokyo's

---

**Gaiatsu*—the Japanese term for "foreign pressure"—is the idea that the only way to get Japan to do something that it does not want to do is for foreign partners to apply enough pressure so that eventually, Japanese decision-makers relent.

**Aspiring sincerely to an international peace based on justice and order, the Japanese people forever renounce war as a sovereign right of the nation and the threat or use of force to settle international disputes. In order to accomplish the aim of the preceding paragraph, land, sea, and air forces, as well as another war potential, will never be maintained. The right of belligerency of the state will not be recognized.

post-war policy in the same way that the 1991 Persian Gulf war rattled the political ranks of Japan.[12] Tokyo is keeping a close watch on Germany, a World War Two ally that adopted pacifist policies similar to Japan post-war. Germany has made some tectonic moves in response to the Russian aggression. It has validated the decades of consensus on defence spending, direct diplomatic intervention in the war, and the nature of countries' ties with Russia.

Four days into the war, German Chancellor Olaf Scholz announced a vast increase in military spending.[13] The decision appears to be backed by the German public that has long been indifferent to defence structural change as its political leaders have several times failed to meet NATO (North Atlantic Treaty Organization) spending commitments.[14] Scholz has already played his offensive cards by promising state-of-the-art weapons to Ukraine in the fight against Moscow's war.[15] This move broke with the longstanding tradition of Germany's pacifism in international diplomacy and could have ripple effects across the European Union.

Tokyo cannot remain untouched by the seismic shift triggered by the geopolitical turmoil in Ukraine. The recent manoeuvring by the Japanese government has raised the eyebrows of many Western powers as it sets precedents for Russia and China's status quo-changing behaviours. When asked whether Tokyo plans to ramp up its security policy and defence spending at a recent conference, Japanese Prime Minister Fumio Kishida answered, 'Japan needs to implement a fundamental upgrade of its defence capabilities'.[16] The demands to give more teeth to defence come against the backdrop of concerns that military and security tensions could rise in North-East Asia following Russia's invasion of Ukraine.

In an interview, US Ambassador to Japan Rahm Emanuel said, 'PM Kishida has stepped up in the geopolitics ladder and stepped onto the global stage in a significant way'.[17] Tokyo is responding to the worldwide crisis on a scale with a speed that the world has never seen earlier. This makes a big difference in showing any intolerance in the change of territorial sovereignty. This has also made the opposition or Russia's expansionist aim not just European but also global.

The Japanese assertiveness is made possible by the years and a decade of LDP leaders, in which former prime minister Shinzo Abe played a prominent role.[18] He cemented the roots of a new Japan, where its foreign and defence policy ushers in incumbent leaders like Fumio Kishida.

Kishida follows the strategic map inherited from Abe. Shinzo Abe's years of efforts worked restlessly to strengthen and deepen Japan's ties with countries in Asia-Pacific and Europe. Those efforts increased vehemently when the USA took the inward-looking approach on the global stage during the 'America First' Donald Trump era. Then, Tokyo began to clearly articulate its foreign policy values in the relative absence or abandonment concerns of its biggest security ally, the USA.[19] Tokyo has been harvesting the benefits of investing in its Western and European diplomacy in the past decade, mainly as it took a more assertive role in sustaining the post-war order in the absence of the USA.

Many in Japan opine that the country's bold actions underscore its resolve to remain a steadfast all-weather ally of the USA. Despite the shock over Biden's withdrawal of American forces from Afghanistan[20] and Washington's pulling out of a significant trade agreement that it brokered in the Indo-Pacific region, only to come at a vague economic framework. From the recent sanctions regime imposed by Japan and allying with its Western friends, Tokyo has gradually learned to be vocal and set diplomatic precedents, articulate its state values, and position Japan's stance on world issues. Japan is setting an example of proactive diplomacy to maintain the international world order.

Recently, Japan's approach had dramatically shifted from its diplomatic posture of 2014 when Russia annexed Crimea. At that time, Tokyo reluctantly agreed to join the Western nations on sanctions out of concern for its reproach with Moscow to resolve a longstanding territorial dispute, which is now in the back seat.[21]

The decades of an old dispute between Japan and Russia are far from over. The idea of regaining Japan's long-lost 'northern territories' appeals to the LDP faction of the government. Tokyo refers to the islands as the Northern Territories and insists on a peace treaty with Russia that would result in Russia's return of at least two of the four islands to Japan. At the same time, the Kremlin keeps militarising the disputed territory. After eight years of tough diplomacy, Moscow explicitly hardened its stance by revising the constitution to ban any territorial concessions to foreign countries.[22] This should have dashed the hopes of many Japanese policymakers. Ironically, longstanding inconclusive talks on solving the dispute and signing a peace treaty from World War II have been suspended. For now, Tokyo has put the peace talks on hold. The Russian invasion has deepened Japan's fear that without a robust, coherent response alongside the G7 significant economies, it risks encouraging Beijing's growing assertiveness and the worsening relationship between Taiwan and China.

Japanese Sanctions

The Japanese sanctions regime and its stiffened resolve against Russia come with a price. Japan's imposition of sanctions on Moscow is almost certainly the final nail in Tokyo's ambition to resume control of its northern disputed Kuril Islands. PM Kishida was swift to follow in the footsteps of most Western nations in the aftermath of Russia's invasion of Ukraine by imposing strict restrictions on several Russian banks and supporting Moscow's removal from the SWIFT (Society for Worldwide Interbank Financial Telecommunications) banking system. Compared to the Japanese sanctions in 2014, Tokyo's response then to the Russian land grab was lukewarm because Japanese Prime Minister Shinzo Abe wanted to avoid antagonising Putin. Even Belarus could not escape the Japanese sanctions. Kishida government sanctions designated individuals and entities, including the President of Belarus, Lukashenko. Additionally, Japan imposed stricter export control measures against Belarus to dent the economy based on Western sanctions.

Announcing the sanctions, Fumio Kishida pointed out that the invasion of Ukraine by Moscow was an attempt to change the status quo by military force, which shook the foundation of rule-based international order. It violates international law that cannot be tolerated and is severely condemned.[23] Tokyo has frozen the assets of multiple senior Russian officials, including President Putin.[24] Additionally, Japan provided loans to Ukraine of around $ 100 million and another $ 100 million in humanitarian assistance.[25]

In addition, Tokyo will prohibit the export of state-of-the-art technology to Moscow, such as semiconductors, and has presented a symbolic list of Russian security entities banned from accessing Japanese exports of any kind.[26] Further, the Japanese government allowed 120 Japan-based Ukrainian citizens holding temporary visas to extend their stay in Japan. In short, Russians crossing the frontier of Ukraine acted as a catalyst in uniting countries against Putin's aggression. This also prompted the Japanese Prime Minister Fumio Kishida to drop the traditional risk-averse decision-making style, including Tokyo's pacifist prudent balancing act, vis-à-vis Russia.

Japan's dependency on Russia for its energy security is not as stark as that of the European nations. However, Tokyo's reliance on fossil fuels has increased following the deadly disaster at the Fukushima nuclear power plant in 2011. As of today, seven nuclear reactors are still in operation in Japan.[27] At the same time, the Japanese energy consumption relies on fossil fuel imports for as much as 90 per cent. The total imports of Russian gas account for a mere 6.5 per cent. Russian natural gas, oil, and coal imports account for 8.7 per cent, 4 per cent, and 10.2 per cent, respectively.[28] Western sanctions, such as Shell's decision to divest from the famed Sakhalin-II LNG pipeline project in Moscow with Tokyo, will be brutal for the Japanese corporate and business fraternity.[29] It constitutes the main route for gas imports from Russia, and walking out of the project will come with a significant price tag.

One vital instance to notice in the paradigm of Japan's response to the present crisis is the Japanese domestic outpouring of support for Ukraine, which highlights the radical shift of Japan from the previous situation of the Crimea annexation, including the withdrawal from Afghanistan and providing domestic support for Japan's assertive approach in its foreign policy realm.[30] The Japanese regime and the common public also set a precedent for any aggressive behaviour of expansionist power in the Indo-Pacific region.

De-securitization of Japan mobilised public opinion

Japanese public opinion has demonstrated full support for war-inflicted Ukraine's plight. This mainly stems from the northern territorial disputes and historical grievances against the Soviet Union dating back to the end of World War II. The last-minute Russian declaration of war on the East Asian nation in August 1945 allowed for the incorporation of territories north of Hokkaido: What Tokyo refers to as the 'northern territories' Russia holds it to be the 'Southern Kurils'. While Moscow's claims are bolstered by international law and effective control, Japan perceives annexation as a historical injustice. Japanese mistrust is augmented by trials and tribunals encountered by temporal Japanese prisoners-of-war in Soviet labour camps.[31]

China remains the pressing security challenge to Japan. However, it is not only about Russia. A recent survey published by Nikkei Asia demonstrates how 77 per cent of Japanese respondents have apprehensions over the adverse effects on Taiwan of Moscow's invasion of Ukraine . The study also highlights much more substantial support than the 2014 Crimea annexation.[32] It is worth comprehending that the concrete actions of citizens have matched these sentiments: Japan witnessed a rapid increase of donations to support Ukraine's cause to volunteers, mainly from Japan Self Defence forces willing to join the 'international brigade' set of Ukraine.[33–35]

The geopolitical ball game in Eastern Europe has led to the realisation that Japan cannot take its national security for granted. Many in Japan now believe they could see a 'unilateral change to the status quo by coercion and force, according to Kishida, in Tokyo's immediate neighborhood.[36] The bravery of the Ukrainian military has spurred a rare philosophical debate within Japan about what the country should prepare to fight. For decades, Tokyo kept a significant self-imposed restriction on its security policy. However, in recent times, Japan has witnessed a security paradigm change.

The existing explanation typically sees them as a response to objectively existing or constructed external threats;[37,38] in this case, the rise of China in Tokyo's backyard and recent apprehension of Russia's aggression. Such threat construction has led to a change in Japan's security outlook. However, it does not fully account for how the previously limited conditions have now contributed to the renaissance of Japanese military doctrine.[39,40] This new wave of confidence among the ordinary Japanese citizens and the state is attributed to the de-securitisation of the Japanese post-war identity, in this case, the *'temporal other'*. In the post-war period, Japan's temporal other was securitised, i.e., they were viewed as an existential threat (Imperial Japan) within Japan and outside.[41] Therefore, Japan followed the pacifist path for long. Thus, bolder security changes did not happen. Additionally, citizens preferred a non-armed Japan after World War II.

More recently, however, de-securitisation of the Japanese temporal other is taking place so that it is no longer seen as a threat domestically and by most other states.[41,42] The speech of Fumio Kishida supporting the Western sanctions regime and criticising Putin's aggression played an essential role in the domestic de-securitisation process by repeating and strengthening the narrative about how Japan was different from *its post-war and cold war others*. The threat emanating from the revival of imperial Japan, which was previously posted by Japan's temporal other, became de-securitised as Japan came to be understood as inherently peaceful, democratic, and a state believing in an international order based on law. These developments have strengthened and mobilised public opinion and the Tokyo regime to go all out in its offensive against Russian aggression.

Conclusion: Motivations and Limitations

Multiple factors combine to motivate Japan's response and offer insights into the limitations of generalising from the present crisis to predict Japan's reaction to other similar concerns.

First, the nature of the conflict and scale differ dramatically from the 2014 Russian annexation of Crimea or in similar cases where Japan showed hesitancy. Currently, the war situation is ambiguous; the conflict is far more brutal and intense, and Moscow's role as an aggressor is undeniable. Nevertheless, Ukraine's resistance in the face of military invasion has attracted and inspired sympathy from the public and governments worldwide, including growing numbers of the Japanese population. Poll data suggests that the proportion of Japanese supporting alignment with the Western sanctions has increased from 43 per cent in January 2022 to 61 per cent in late February 2022 after the conflict's inception.[43,44]

Second, Moscow's action undermines the norms governing the international world order. Suppose a state like Russia violates the fundamental principle of territorial sovereignty without facing the consequences. In that case, it destabilises the roots of international relations in a way that threatens Tokyo's national interests, potentially jeopardising parallels to revisionist China, political elites and Japanese citizens. As Kishida declared, Japan has been a beneficiary of the post-world war order and, over the past years, has taken a responsible role in defending its institutions and principles for promoting a free and open Indo-Pacific region.

Third, while it was a common tradition to treat Europe and Asia as separate, the importance of developments in one region affecting the other areas is well understood from the Ukrainian crisis. Japan welcomes increased engagement by the European nations in the Indo-Pacific region to build coalitions with like-minded partners to address and resolve regional problems. By displaying strong solidarity with Ukraine and Europe, Japan amplified the effect of the sanctions of other countries, signalling to its European partners in the hope that, in a contingency, they will reciprocate in the event of similar turmoil in the Indo-Pacific region, such as the South China Sea issue of Taiwan.

Fourth, the essential aspect argues that the de-securitisation of Japan's temporal other is taking place, where its neighbouring states do not perceive Japan as a threat through the speech of Fumio Kishida. This has resulted in changes in the Japanese security policy. Re-articulating Japanese statements supporting Ukraine and setting precedents for status quo-changing behaviour has played a crucial role. Such ideas have played a vital role in the repetition of the de-securitising narrative. The argument is not that these statements have merely caused policy changes but that they have also contributed to enabling them.

Finally, Japan will likely endorse a value-based foreign policy and continue its traditional pragmatic approach. When the nature of conflict is ambiguous, or Japan's economic stake is higher, Japan is likely to display some hesitancy due to economic interdependence. Even with Ukraine, it remains to be seen how far the West will go with the sanctions and to what extent Tokyo will follow. While the eastern European crisis may not herald a sea of changes in the overall Japanese security architecture, it does make a turning point in policy towards China and Russia. Japan's action so far reveals some latent differences in how Tokyo perceives its role and its willingness to confront new traditional and non-traditional security changes.

ENDNOTES

1. BBC. Japan election: PM Fumio Kishida declares victory for ruling LDP, BBC News. https://www.bbc.com/news/world-asia-59110828 (2022).
2. Hughes, C.W. Japan's "resentful realism" and balancing China's rise. *Chinese Journal of International Politics*, 9, 109–150 (2016).
3. Miao, J. Securing the Status Quo: Contesting Interests and Discourses in the East and South China Sea and Sino Japan Relations. *Journal of Asia-Pacific Studies* (2018).
4. House of Representatives Japan. Resolution condemning Russia's aggression against Ukraine. *Diet* https://www.shugiin.go.jp/internet/itdb_english.nsf/html/statics/english/ketugi_e220301-1.html (2022).

5. Gale, A. Japan Will Send the Ukrainian Military Basic Supplies. https://www.wsj.com/livecoverage/russia-ukraine-latest-news-2022-03-04/card/japan-will-send-the-ukrainian-military-basic-supplies-VOtpnPjTX2ooK8dqQ8o8 (2022).
6. Ministry of Defence. Transportation of bulletproof vests, helmets, etc. for Ukraine, Japan Ministry of Defence. https://www.mod.go.jp/en/article/2022/03/0b5ad4b67f12207d092b8f7f27999dee1109ab5b.html (2022).
7. The Japan Times. In rare move, Japan to send bulletproof vests and helmets to Ukraine, *The Japan Times*. https://www.japantimes.co.jp/news/2022/03/04/national/sdf-vests-helmets-ukraine/ (2022).
8. Miyashita, A. Gaiatsu and Japan's Foreign Aid: Rethinking the Reactive-Proactive Debate. *International Studies Quarterly*, 43, 695–731 (1999).
9. Nadeau, P. The End of Gaiatsu? Centre for Strategic and International Studies. https://www.csis.org/analysis/end-gaiatsu (2018).
10. McNelly, T. The Renunciation of War in the Japanese Constitution. *Political Science Quarterly*, 77, 350 (1962).
11. Michelle Ye Hee Lee. Japan's foreign policy grows more assertive after Ukraine invasion, *The Washington Post*. https://www.washingtonpost.com/world/2022/03/05/japan-ukraine-russia-foreign-policy/ (2022).
12. Catalinac, A. L. Identity Theory and Foreign Policy: Explaining Japan's Responses to the 1991 Gulf War and the 2003 U.S. War in Iraq. *Politics & Policy*, 35, 58–100 (2007).
13. Jean Pisani-Ferry. The economic policy consequences of the war. - Document - Gale Academic OneFile. *Bruegel* https://go.gale.com/ps/i.do?id=GALE%7CA696208490&sid=googleScholar&v= 2.1&it=r&linkaccess=abs&issn=&p=AONE&sw=w&userGroupName=anon%7Ec6910499 (2022).
14. Eloranta, J. From the great illusion to the Great War: Military spending behaviour of the Great Powers, 1870–1913. *European Review of Economic History*, 11, 255–283 (2007).
15. Antezza, A. *et al.* EconStor: Which countries help Ukraine and how? Introducing the Ukraine Support Tracker. *Kiel Institute for the World Economy (IfW Kiel)*, Kiel https://www.econstor.eu/handle/10419/253672 (2022).
16. The Mainichi. Editorial: Defence spending hike without any debate puts Japan on precarious course - *The Mainichi* https://mainichi.jp/english/articles/20220603/p2a/00m/0op/027000c (2022).
17. Yoshinari Kurose and Kazuyuki Sakamoto. Interview, US and Japan: Bringing the Transatlantic and Indo-Pacific Together. *Japan Forward*, https://japan-forward.com/interview-us-and-japan-bringing-the-transatlantic-and-indo-pacific-together/ (2022).
18. Kumar, A. New Osake in an old bottle, The new Japanese PM Fumio Kishida. *Centre For Security Studies Issue Brief*, www.cas.go.jp/jp/seisaku/keizai_anzen_hosyohousei/dai4/teigen.pdf. (2022).
19. Solís, M. U.S.-Japan relations in the era of Trump: Navigating the turbulence of "America First". *México y la Cuenca del Pacífico*, 8, 9–17 (2019).
20. Satoh, H. Middle or Muddle: Whither Post-Abe Japan? https://doi.org/10.1142/S1793930522000058, 14, 71–84 (2022).
21. Kamata Tomoko. Japan-Russia peace treaty talks suspended, *NHK-World*, https://www3.nhk.or.jp/nhkworld/en/news/backstories/1958/ (2022).
22. James D. and J. Brown. Russia's Revised Constitution Shows Putin is No Friend of

Japan, Royal United Services Institute. *RUSI* https://rusi.org/explore-our-research/publications/commentary/russias-revised-constitution-shows-putin-no-friend-japan (2022).

23. Michito, T. Why Japan Is Getting Tough on Russia Now, *The Diplomat* https://thediplomat.com/2022/06/why-japan-is-getting-tough-on-russia-now/ (2022).
24. Ukraine: EU excludes 7 Russian banks from SWIFT, News, DW, 02.03.2022. https://www.dw.com/en/ukraine-eu-excludes-7-russian-banks-from-swift/a-60985990.
25. Additional Emergency Humanitarian Assistance in Ukraine and neighbouring countries, Ministry of Foreign Affairs of Japan. https://www.mofa.go.jp/press/release/press4e_003108.html
26. Japan's Sanctions Related to the Situation in Ukraine, White & Case LLP. *White & Case* https://www.whitecase.com/publications/alert/japans-sanctions-related-situation-ukraine (2022).
27. Reuters Staff. TABLE-Japan nuclear reactor operations: Kyushu Electric shuts Sendai No. 2 reactor, *Reuters* https://www.reuters.com/article/japan-nuclear-operations/table-japan-nuclear-reactor-operations-kyushu-electric-shuts-sendai-no-2-reactor-idUSL1N2UZ13P (2022).
28. Takeo Kumagai and Meghan Gordon. Japan does not see sanctions on Russia causing major energy supply disruption, *S&P Global Commodity Insights* https://www.spglobal.com/commodityinsights/en/market-insights/latest-news/oil/022422-japan-does-not-see-sanctions-on-russia-causing-major-disruption-to-energy-supply (2022).
29. James D., J. Brown and William Sposato. Russia's War Ruins Years of Diplomacy by Japan. *Foreign Policy* https://foreignpolicy.com/2022/03/02/japan-ukraine-sanctions/ (2022).
30. Fukumoto, K. and Tabuchi, T. The Rally 'round the Flag Effect in a Third Party: The Japanese Reaction to the Russian Invasion of Ukraine. (2022) doi:10.31235/OSF.IO/U8H6Y
31. Muminov, S. *Eleven winters of discontent/: the Siberian internment and the making of a new Japan*, Harvard University Press, 2022.
32. Ryo Nemoto. Ukraine conflict: 77% in Japan fear Taiwan spillover, *Nikkei Asia* https://asia.nikkei.com/Politics/Ukraine-conflict-77-in-Japan-fear-Taiwan-spillover (2022).
33. Donations for Ukrainians Increasing Rapidly in Japan, Nippon.com. *Jiji Press* https://www.nippon.com/en/news/yjj2022030200258/ (2022).
34. Yoshikatsu Nakajima. Rakuten CEO Mikitani to donate 1 billion yen to Ukraine | Breaking News, Japan News and Analysis. *The Asahi Shimbun* https://www.asahi.com/ajw/articles/14560885 (2022).
35. Yusuke Kaite and Shu Hatakeyama. 70 Japanese apply to become volunteer soldiers in Ukraine, many ex-SDF personnel, *The Mainichi* https://mainichi.jp/english/articles/20220302/p2a/00m/0na/007000c (2022).
36. TsuruokaMichito. Why Japan Is Getting Tough on Russia Now, *The Diplomat* https://thediplomat.com/2022/06/why-japan-is-getting-tough-on-russia-now/ (2022).
37. Oren, E. and Brummer, M. Re-examining Threat Perception in Early Cold War Japan. *Journal of Cold War Studies*, 22, 71–112 (2020).
38. Hughes, C.W. *Japan's re-emergence as a "normal" military power*. Routledge, 1–156 (2013) doi:10.4324/9781315000831/JAPAN-RE-EMERGENCE-NORMAL-MILITARY-POWER-CHRISTOPHER-HUGHES.

39. TsuruokaMichito and Keisuke Matsuyama. *Japan's Military Renaissance? Japan's Military Renaissance?*, Palgrave Macmillan UK, 1993. doi:10.1007/978-1-349-22777-8.
40. Ministry of Foreign Affairs of Japan. Security Environment Surrounding Japan and Challenges, Ministry of Foreign Affairs of Japan. *MOEA Japan* https://www.mofa.go.jp/fp/nsp/page1we_000078.html (2016).
41. Gustafsson, K. Temporal othering, de-securitisation and apologies: understanding Japanese security policy change. *Journal of International Relations and Development*, 23, 511–534 (2020).
42. Singh, B. ASEAN's perceptions of Japan: Change and continuity. *Asian Survey*, 42, 276–296 (2002).
43. Nikkei Opinion Poll Archive: Nihon Keizai Shimbun. *Asia Nikkei* https://vdata.nikkei.com/newsgraphics/cabinet-approval-rating/# (2022).
44. Craig Kafura. Japanese Public Backs Sanctions on Russia, Aid to Ukraine, *The Chicago Council on Global Affairs* https://www.thechicagocouncil.org/commentary-and-analysis/blogs/japanese-public-backs-sanctions-russia-aid-ukraine (2022).
45. The Constitution of Japan. https://japan.kantei.go.jp/constitution_and_government_of_japan/constitution_e.html.

CHAPTER 7

The Fourth Front in the Ukraine Conflict: Cyberwarfare and Disinformation Campaigns by Russia and China

Nishant Dilip Sharma

ABSTRACT

Wars traditionally fought on the fronts of land, air, and sea have also transcended into a new front- the digital space. A similar strategy marks Russia's attack on Ukraine in 2022. Attempts were made to gain a strategic advantage in the conflict on the ground, even before troops were physically mobilized. As the conflict progressed, there was visible complementarity in cyber and kinetic activity. Such complementarity is a part of a hybrid form of warfare, which is imbued in the strategic culture of both Russia and China. In the present times, the non-kinetic element of hybrid warfare is often undertaken in the information domain- through disinformation and cyberattacks. Forensic analysis by major companies like Google's Threat Analysis Team, Microsoft, Symantec, and ESET conclude that several cyber-attacks targeted Ukraine's range of critical cyber infrastructures, including civil, military, and government agencies. This chapter argues that the cyberattacks orchestrated on Ukraine's cyberinfrastructure are consistent with a "thunder-run" strategy aimed at bewilderment, chaos, and a swift victory over Ukraine. In addition to these attacks targeting real-world capabilities, information war was also employed to legitimize Russian actions and mould domestic perceptions in the countries concerned. Together, they constitute the fourth front actively manoeuvred by Russia and its silent ally - China. The chapter analyses news reports and social media content promulgated by State-affiliated media in Russia and China and attempts to evaluate the intent and the efficacy of these undertakings. It also aims to characterize China's support to Russia in this conflict and explore its motivations behind complicity in the conflict. The chapter posits that cyberwarfare and disinformation campaigns were used complementarily to limit the on-ground capacity of Ukraine and legitimize Russian actions, respectively.

Keywords: *Cyberwarfare, Disinformation, Thunder-Run Strategy, Russia-China Relations, Hybrid Warfare.*

Introduction

On 13 January 2022, several websites associated with the Ukrainian government were attacked, and a warning appeared on them stating, 'Be afraid and expect the worst'.[1] The notice appeared on several government websites and was written in Ukrainian, Polish, and Russian. The next day, on 14 January, White House Press Secretary Jen Psaki claimed that US Intelligence reports indicated that Russia was laying the groundwork through a social media disinformation campaign designed to frame Ukraine as an aggressor in an attack imminent against the Russian forces in the Eastern region of Ukraine.[2]

These two reports came on the heels of talks between Russia and the USA in Geneva over the issue of Ukraine and NATO. During these talks, the Russian side demanded a binding pledge from the USA and its allies that Ukraine or any other ex-Soviet state would not be incorporated into NATO. With no real progress made during these talks, the cyber attacks ensued, and the intelligence reports on Russian disinformation foreshadowed one of the most significant armed conflicts in recent years—the Ukraine War of 2022.

What followed was an announcement by Russian President Putin during a Security Council meeting on 24 February that Russia was initiating a 'full-scale land, sea, and air invasion of Ukraine targeting Ukrainian military assets and cities across the country.[3] The material damage caused by such kinetic warfare (fought over the three conventional fronts of land, air, and sea) often conceals the activities on the fourth front—the cyber front. It is also essential to study the activities on the fourth front because, as evident with the Ukraine crisis and the Crimean situation, this cyber front gets activated even before actual kinetic warfare starts and often outlasts the withdrawal of the last troops on the ground.

In this chapter, the notion of cyber warfare is employed to incorporate both conventional cyber-attacks and disinformation campaigns. It is argued that both these components of cyber warfare were used not in isolation but following the kinetic warfare occurring on the ground. This chapter focuses on the role of Russia and China in orchestrating such attacks on the fourth front. It evaluates what kind of cyber warfare both countries were involved in and their respective efficacies in achieving the desired goal.

Russia, China, and Hybrid Warfare

Both Russia and China have been accused of using hybrid methods of warfare for political and geostrategic aims. For the Russians, a hybrid means of war is termed *gibridnayavoyna.* There are multiple perceptions concerning the use of this strategy, but there is a consistent inclusion of tactics often observed in the cyber domain and information sphere. For instance, Russian military theorist Vladimirov argues that *gibridnayavoyna* can be viewed as a 'struggle over thoughts, morals, and codices'.[4] This interpretation reveals the importance of disinformation campaigns in the Russian military strategy of hybrid warfare. In another view, Popov and Khamzatov argue that hybrid warfare involves the simultaneous use of irregular and regular forces.[5] The combined use of traditional and irregular forces is comparable to Russia's cyber-attacks in Estonia in 2007, during the Russo-Georgia conflict in 2008, Crimea in 2014, and most recently, in Ukraine in 2022. Since cyber-attacks may involve using state-sponsored hacktivists who are not easy to track, their use as irregular forces becomes highly appealing. Therefore, Russia expected to deploy these irregular forces before the kinetic invasion of Ukraine in 2022. This is precisely the case, as argued in the next section.

For the Chinese, the understanding of hybrid warfare goes as far back as the 5th century BCE, when the classic on warfare, *The Art of War,* was written. The People's Liberation Army (PLA) Daily's senior editor, Major General Li Bingyan, has written extensively on lessons from *The Art of War* and the 'butterfly effect' generated by this hybrid warfare, where interdependence amongst various sectors can be exploited.[6] A more recent work by two Chinese generals called *Unrestricted Warfare* has contributed to the modern discourses of hybrid warfare in China.[7] Saalman argues that this form of 'unrestricted warfare', which employs all means to compel the enemy into accepting one's interests, fits well into China's conception of 'continuous revolution' practised at home and abroad.[8]

This 'continuous revolution' is also perceived as a bid to replace the USA as the pre-eminent superpower and restore China's place as the 'Middle Kingdom', not just in the East but also across the globe.[9] Many of China's hybrid operations are directed at the USA, with cyber-enabled intellectual property theft irritating. Its information operations have already spread globally, with many Confucius Institutes acting as conduits of cultural influence.[10] Additionally, China has invested significantly in media companies in foreign nations that purposefully shape narratives in line with Chinese national interests.[11] Although information operations form a significant component of Chinese hybrid warfare, there are reports of Chinese-operated cyber-attacks on countries with which it has conflicts. In 2021, reports surfaced of Chinese hackers targeting civilian organizations in many Southeast Asian nations, particularly those involved in a dispute with China over the South China Sea issue.[12]

Since both China and Russia share a similar worldview, with the USA perceived as an aggressor, cooperation in a conflict affecting either of the parties becomes more likely. The possibility of such collaboration increases with the 'no limits partnership' announced on 4 February. Therefore, it is pertinent to look at the Russian and Chinese actions during the Russian invasion of Ukraine in 2022.

Cyber-attacks preceding the invasion

Several attacks were initiated in January and February this year on government and civilian organizations. Notably, many of these attacks were undertaken during failed diplomatic talks or hostile diplomatic signalling by Russia on Ukraine. For instance, on 13 January 2022, when Russia claimed that a dead-end had been reached on the Ukraine talks during the Organization for Security and Co-operation in Europe (OSCE) meeting in Vienna, two cyber-attacks followed. The first one was malware detected by Microsoft on the same day, referred to as 'WhisperGate'. This malware attacked the Ukrainian government and IT sector systems.[13] It was followed by a Distributed Denial of Service (hereafter referred to as DDoS) attack on the next day, 14 January that targeted government websites in Ukraine. Subsequently, another DDoS attack followed on February 15 and 16, targeting Ukraine's financial institutions.[14] The next day, the Kremlin informed the USA in a document that it would be forced to take 'military-technical' measures if it was not given guarantees that Ukraine would never be admitted to NATO.

Another instance of such coordinated actions occurred within a week when, on 21 February, President Putin recognized the separatist regions of Donetsk and Luhansk. Two days later, on the 23rd, two new wiper families were detected by ESET targeting Ukrainian organizations.[15] These wipers were essential 'data-wiping' tools hitting hundreds of computers in Ukraine. According to Guerrero-Saade, a cyber-security researcher at Sentinel One, this attack could only have been possible if the hackers already possessed domain admin control, in effect, owning the entire enterprise. Therefore, such an attack could only be seen as attempting to 'damage, disable, signal, and cause havoc'.[16] Though these attacks lack a credible attribution, they can be seen acting as per Russian statecraft on the Ukraine issue.

The Hybrid Thunder-Run and its failure

The Thunder Run strategy is generally discussed in the context of kinetic warfare. From the Vietnam war to the Gulf wars, military strategists have regularly used the term to convey acts of sudden and swift operations. These operations ranged from armoured convoys canvassing lands for mines in Vietnam to the blitz on Korean army personnel returning after payday.[17] However, the most discussed iteration comes from American operations in the Iraqi war, where a series of swift attacks were initiated targeting Baghdad's defences for a speedy victory. A similar attempt marks the aims of the Russian 'special military operation' in Ukraine. Hoping for a swift success and avoiding a protracted war, Russia initiated a strategy similar to the kinetic thunder run, albeit a hybrid one. This hybrid strategy involved cyber-attacks on government, military, critical services, and border control stations, while simultaneous attacks continued on the ground as part of kinetic warfare. Cattler and Black[18] argue that these attacks are 'entirely consistent with a so-called thunder run strategy intended to stoke chaos, confusion, and uncertainty, and ultimately avoid a costly and protracted war in Ukraine.'

A report published by Microsoft's Digital Security Unit (Figure 7.1) confirms this claim. The report claims that a timeline of military strikes and cyber intrusions between late February and early April indicate that both 'seemingly worked in tandem against a shared target set'.[19]

Another argument for the thunder-run strategy can be found in a paper written by Singaporean Major Goh Si Mien, who argues that the

Figure 7.1: Cyber intrusions and military strikes: Russia's invasion of Ukraine

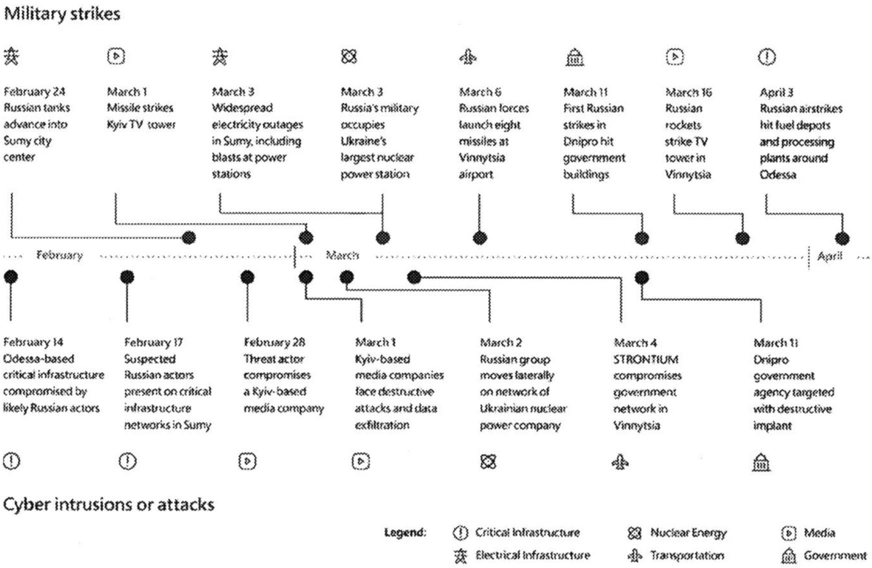

Source: Special Report on Ukraine, Digital Information Unit, Microsoft (2022).

intent behind a thunder-run system is to 'thrust a sizeable force in the heart of the enemy's nerve centre'.[20] Taking the example of Baghdad, he argues that such attacks are undertaken more prominently in areas of a higher population density and where major critical infrastructure is located. Looking at Figure 7.2 published by Microsoft's Digital Security Unit, one can observe areas with high kinetic and cyber activity complementarity between 23 February and 6 April. For instance, regions around Kyiv Oblast and Kharkiv Oblast—the two most densely populated areas in Ukraine—also observed high amounts of both kinetic and cyber activities.

However, despite evidence that suggests the cyber-attacks made on Ukraine were well planned, targeted, and coordinated, there is little doubt that these activities failed to achieve the strategic objectives. There are several reasons why Russia failed on the first part of the cyber front. As argued by several experts, the attacks were not as disruptive as expected. There could be two reasons for this visible restraint and targeting choices. The first concerns Russia's need to avail of the Ukrainian infrastructure

Figure 7.2: Cyber and Kinetic Activity: Russia's invasion of Ukraine

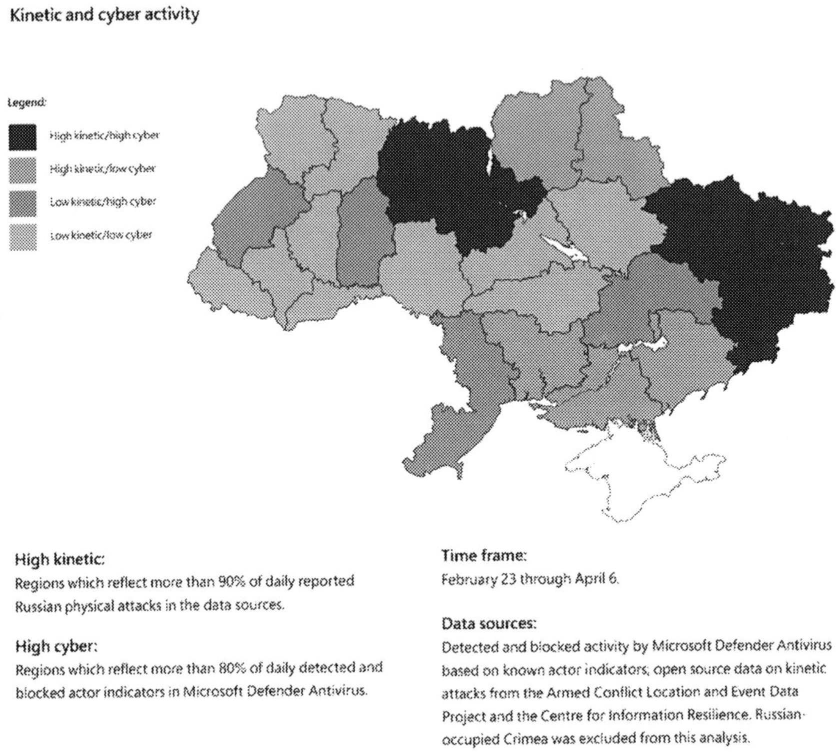

Source: Special Report on Ukraine, Digital Information Unit, Microsoft (2022).

to support their stretched supply lines. With these supply lines constantly under attack by Ukrainian civilians,[21] a lack of access to Ukraine's infrastructure could deter a full-scale disruption. In addition, another reason for restraining visible large-scale disturbances could be Putin's fear of NATO retaliation. If such an attack is successfully attributed to Russia, it could invoke the collective defence clause of NATO. In his interaction with Reuters, NATO's Deputy Secretary-General and an unnamed official made such warnings public. The unnamed official also stated that determining if a cyber-attack met the threshold of invoking Article 5 was a 'political decision for NATO Allies to make'.[22]

Another reason for the failure of the thunder-run is the counter-offensive launched by the Ukrainian and global army of cyber hacktivists who took the offensive against Russia. Following the invasion, several 'hacktivist' groups have hacked into dozens of Russian institutions, targeting mainly those associated with the Kremlin's internet censor and state media corporations.[23] Lastly, the failed hybrid thunder-run strategy could also result from a wartime allure of using conventional weapons for a more direct, effective and lasting strike. It could be that the Russians overestimated their conventional arsenal's efficacy at crucial stages of the war.

Conceptualizing Disinformation

The use of information to mislead, cause harm, deceive, and polarize comes in various forms. Disinformation is often confused with misinformation. It can be defined as a more severe and dangerous form of information manipulation since it is intentional and purposive. On the other hand, misinformation can be inadvertently shared as false information that may not be intended to cause harm.[24] However, as Fallis[25] notes, all disinformation cannot be equated with lies. Some forms of disinformation may consist of truthful information but aim to portray a distorted view of reality. In the larger scheme of things, disinformation as a part of cyber warfare consists of propaganda campaigns employed to manipulate online discourses. As we shall see in this chapter, this form of disinformation aptly characterizes the CCP's attempt at information manipulation within China.

Though disinformation features consistently in most political discourses, its utility is compounded at the time of war. Sun Tzu famously argued that 'all warfare is based on deception'.[26] When discussed in the context of war, disinformation presents itself in three interrelated concepts—war propaganda, psychological operations, and hybrid warfare.[27] War propaganda and psychological warfare are targeted at enemy morale, and information is used as a tool. However, hybrid warfare is unique in that it employs various instruments of power simultaneously, including military, political, economic, civil, and information. When a country undertakes hybrid warfare, there is a more excellent synchronization of these instruments of control.[28]

As a logical extension, it is expected that a disinformation campaign undertaken as part of hybrid warfare will show a greater level of synchronization with other instruments of power. This is markedly so in the context of the Ukraine war. Russia pulled multiple levers simultaneously while unleashing the might of its military on Ukraine. In terms of scope, disinformation employed abroad and at home has two separate but interrelated practical utilities. Disinformation used abroad can be seen as a tool of public diplomacy wherein resources are mobilized to communicate with people of other nations or, more broadly, manage the state's soft power.

On the other hand, disinformation employed at home is generally used for bolstering regime legitimacy and popular support. Both Russia and China took great pains to ensure that the domestic perception of the war favoured Russian moves. Quite naturally for Putin, the disinformation campaigns at home were necessary to justify a largely unprovoked war. For China, the reasons were different. China's disinformation within the mainland was directed in favour of Russia for two possible explanations. The first one concerns avoiding a 'loss of face' in the aftermath of announcing a 'no limits friendship' just weeks before the Ukrainian invasion began. The second reason could be the projection of a familiar 'strategic encirclement' narrative at home, which China faces in the Indo-Pacific.

The role of Neo-Nazi propaganda in enabling the 'special operation'

One of the primary justifications for Russia's use of force against Ukraine has been its narrative of de-nazifying Ukraine.[29] Putin has tried to invoke the memory of fighting fascism during the second world war and has ceaselessly used the slur of Nazism against Ukraine. This categorization is not new, as Russia has been employing the narrative of fascism and Nazism in the context of Ukraine for long. Most of the pro-West Ukrainians are brandished as 'Banderites', a term that has been in use since the 1980s to vilify Ukrainian nationalists by the Soviet Union.[30] The word comes from the legacy of Stepan Bandera, a nationalist leader from the 1920s until his assassination in the late 1950s. Under Bandera's leadership, the Organization of Ukrainian Nationalists (OUN) infamously collaborated with Nazi Germany during the Second World War and was complicit in the ethnic cleansing of Jews in Poland. The recent resurrection of Bandera's legacy has only added fuel to Russia's propaganda. In addition to this convoluted history, the 2014 Maidan revolt and the subsequent power transition towards a pro-Western government made the narrative against

Kyiv even more vitriolic. Russia-backed rebellion in the eastern Donbas region has been branded as a fight to liberate the area from Ukrainian Nazis who have occupied the territory by force.

The disinformation campaigns have continued despite the Ukrainian President being a democratically elected Jew. The result of this campaign seems mixed at best. To assess the efficacy of this campaign, one must answer which audience is the neo-nazi rhetoric directed at. The most plausible answer would be that it is directed inward. At the same time, there are several ways to deflect diplomatic imputations, including NATO expansionism, dominance of the USA, and Western collusion; rhetoric for domestic audiences needs to be more 'effective'. Neo-Nazi propaganda fills that gap and procures enough public support for the 'special military operation'. According to a study by the Levada Center, this move seems to have led to fruition in garnering the required public support. According to their research, an overwhelming majority (81%) of the Russian populace surveyed support the Russian armed action in Ukraine.[31]

Figure 7.3: Russian population's support or disregard of the invasion of Ukraine

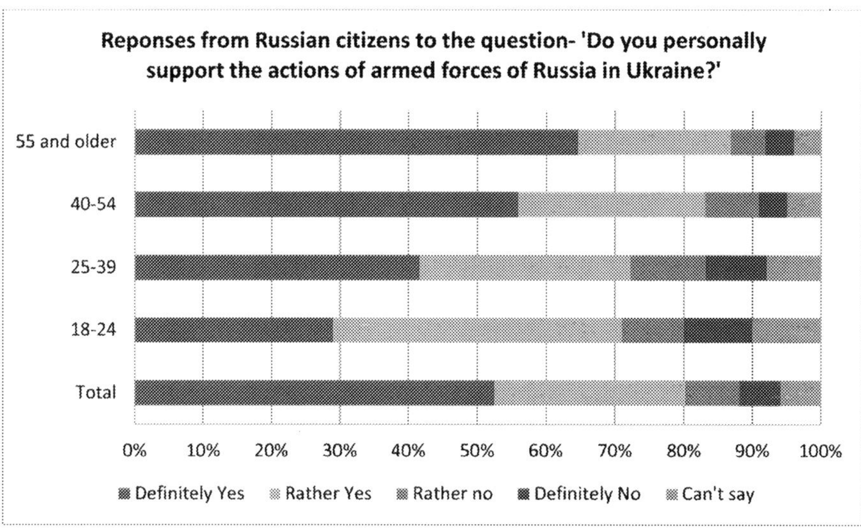

Source: The Levada Center, https://www.levada.ru/en/2022/04/11/the-conflict-with-ukraine

China's Role in the Fourth Front

There are differing views on China's complicity or knowledge of the impending Russian invasion of Ukraine at the time of Putin's visit to China for the Winter Olympics 2022. Some reports suggested that China knew of the attack, and senior Chinese officials asked Russian officials to stall the invasion till the end of the Winter Olympics in Beijing.[32] However, signing the 'no limits' joint statement on 4 February casts doubts on such a claim. Had China known and still agreed to the report, it would imply direct complicity in the invasion. The Joint Statement opposed the expansion of NATO and the formation of bloc structures.[33] China also supported the Russian demand for a legally binding security guarantee in Europe. After the invasion began, China's ambivalent diplomatic positioning and lack of military support indicate that China did not wish to appear hand in hand with Russia's cause.

Nevertheless, China did not abandon Russia in a war emanating from a shared worldview. Outside the multilateral forums, China's position has been markedly pro-Russian. China has emerged as Russia's biggest ally in the fourth front. Some claim that cyber groups linked to the Chinese government launched cyber-attacks against Ukraine's police agencies to gather information on Ukrainian refugees.[34] Although direct attribution remains a problem, there is ample evidence of a Russia-China alliance on the disinformation front. China's echoing of Russian messaging is evident on Western platforms (such as Twitter), domestic social media platforms, and state media. China's support for Russia on the informational front can be best described as 'disinformation surrogacy'. Like a surrogate, China has pushed the Russian agenda without any modification or modulation in most cases. There are several ways in which this has been executed:

1. **Adoption of Russian disinformation without fact-check**
   The Chinese state media has been adopting Russian propaganda without due fact-checking. There are several instances where information brazenly untrue has been popularized to support the Russian narrative. On February 24, *Global Times* posted a manipulated video giving the impression that Ukrainian troops were laying down their arms in large numbers. This was adopted directly from the Russian state-controlled television network, RT.[35] Two days later, Chinese media outlets claimed that Ukrainian President Volodymyr

Zelensky had fled the capital. This claim was sourced from Russian State Duma and published without internal verification. A similar example of disinformation pushed across Weibo was a video claiming that Zelensky was abusing drugs while the crisis unfolded. This video was later flagged as doctored by Politico.[36] Another piece of disinformation perhaps best suited for consumption in Chinese media was the claim that the Russians had discovered biolabs in Ukraine.

In a study conducted by US-China Perception Monitor, when respondents were asked about their familiarity with the biolabs theory, almost half responded that they had seen it before. Amongst those who reported having seen the information before, a large fraction (72%) was convinced that the information was accurate.[37] Such conspicuous adoption of disinformation is facilitated by several agreements signed between Russian and Chinese news sources. Since 2014, Russia's *Sputnik News, China Media Group, Xinhua News Agency, Chinese Radio International*, and *Global Times* have entered into multiple agreements that facilitate content sharing and joint projects.[38] Deals like these between like-minded autocratic states serve to seep a consonant and sympathetic narrative across the borders. Therefore, it is no surprise that there is often a high sense of support within the Chinese public towards Russia. In the survey conducted by US-China Perception Monitor, two-thirds of the Chinese citizens surveyed agreed that supporting Russia was in China's best interests.

2. Conflict framing suited to Russian interests

While there is a resounding consensus in the Western conception of the war being a unilateral act of aggression, the conflict has been framed differently in Chinese media and state-affiliated social media handles. According to a study by Alliance for Securing Democracy, Chinese state media and government officials have preferred the term 'special military operation' over words like 'invasion' to describe the war in Ukraine. Their study has revealed that between 24 February and 12 March, the term 'special military operation' was used 180 times, while the word 'invasion' was used 145 times on Twitter by Chinese-affiliated accounts. Amongst the 145 times that the word 'invasion' was used, more than a third of the mentions were related to the US invasions, not Russian.[39] This framing did alter when Wang Yi interacted with the Ukrainian Foreign Minister. According to Reuters,

Wang, in his interaction with Dmytro Kuleba, passively acknowledged the existence of war while stating, 'Wars end eventually. The key is how to reflect on the pain, to maintain lasting security in Europe and establish a balanced, effective and sustainable European security mechanism'.[40] It is worth noting here that Wang's acknowledgement of the existence of a 'war' came at a time when it was struggling to evacuate Chinese citizens from Ukraine amid a hostile sentiment there against the Chinese. Considering the context, the feigned remark can only be seen as opportunist by the Chinese.

A more sincere framing to characterize this conflict would have been to accept that it is an invasion. However, China is bound by its historical commitment to the non-endorsement of using force against sovereign nations to acknowledge such a framing. This shows that it is not atypical for China to honour its bilateral relations (in this case, the no-limits partnership) over long-nurtured positions in diplomatic conduct. To argue that is also a case of short-term thinking over long-term posturing is not so straightforward. Given the current trend of great power politics, it can be asserted that siding with Russia has more long-term benefits. This thinking is also evident in a tweet by Chinese journalist Liu Xin, in which she mocked the proposition of condemning Russia in an oblique expression, 'Can you help me fight your friend so that I can concentrate on fighting you later?'[41]

3. **Suppression of information that provides a narrative counter to Russian interests**
   Promoting the pro-Russian narrative in China is accompanied by a robust censorship regime cracking down on any expression of sentiment diverging from the official record. In March, a leak containing censorship instructions was distributed online. This leak by the Cyberspace Administration of China instructed media platforms to 'turn down the temperature toward the Russia-Ukraine conflict' and 'control pessimism about Sino-Russian relations'. The resultant coverage has diluted facts and often presents a one-sided picture. Similarly, Sarah Cook claims that amidst the disinformation propagated there is a void where basic facts are missing. Basic information such as that Moscow initiated the war in violation of international law is missing. In addition, videos of President Zelensky, which have otherwise gone viral on Western social media, have

received no airtime on the Chinese media. She adds that the prime-time CCTV coverage also avoided reporting civilian deaths reported in Bucha in early April.[42]

4. **Whataboutism targeted the West and the USA in particular**
Chinese media and state officials have not gone amiss on the opportunity of raising counter-accusations against the USA and the West on their questionable record in regions such as Afghanistan, Iraq, Libya, Serbia, and Yemen. This propaganda technique, known as Whataboutism in political discourses, is often used to deflect criticism by discrediting the accuser. This is achieved by turning the criticism back on the accuser and is known as *tu quoque* (Latin for 'you also').[43] Chinese whataboutism has targeted the USA on its double standards by using the State media to propagate videos. For example, CGTN affiliate T-House published an old video where Biden is confronted by an Iraq war veteran over his role in facilitating the Iraq war, which led to thousands of civilian deaths and casualties of armed personnel.[44] Such campaigns are designed to draw attention away from the crisis unfolding in real-time and create a sense of apathy towards the issues at hand. Exposing the 'Western Hypocrisy' has become the perfect tool to hide Russian human rights abuses behind the shroud of Whataboutry.

Although it is difficult to quantify the efficacy of these counter-narratives, there is evidence that shows the Chinese people can see through the narrative, at least when it directly concerns them. Amid the war, when CGTN started a trend which roughly translates to 'USA is the worst country when it comes to human rights', the movement was quickly overtaken by Chinese netizens eager to voice their concerns regarding the deteriorating COVID situation. After the initial bouts of tweets targeting the USA, the hashtag was quickly adopted with texts facetiously criticizing the USA accompanied by pictures showcasing discontent with Chinese policies.[45]

5. **Blaming NATO and the USA as the aggressor**
Amongst all the narratives adopted by China in the context of the Russia-Ukraine crisis, perhaps the most sustained and consistent has been one blaming the USA and NATO for the current state of affairs. This narrative has been consistent across all channels, both domestic

> and abroad. Multiple commentaries have been published in the *People's Daily* that vilified the USA's role and blamed its policies as the root cause of the conflict. In one such commentary series, Zhong Sheng, a piece claims that the USA bears an 'unshrinkable responsibility' for the war. It also adds that 'the USA-led NATO's eastward expansion is at the root of the Ukrainian crisis'.[46]

Such a narrative serves two essential purposes for China. On the one hand, it vindicates Russia, furthering the 'no limits partnership'; additionally, it helps to promote the narrative that a similar encirclement strategy is being attempted concerning China. China's geostrategic imperatives are identical to Russia's, with QUAD replacing NATO, Taiwan replacing Ukraine, and the USA being the same geostrategic competitor in both cases.

Conclusion

Several observations can be made in the light of the evidence presented in this chapter on the fourth front in the Ukraine conflict. It can be safely concluded that there was a fourth front in this conflict, apart from the conventional shows of land, air, and sea. Both Russia and China participated in the front but in different capacities. Since Russia was the aggressor in this conflict and a direct party, greater cyber-attacks were initiated at its behest to target multiple sectors of the Ukrainian digital infrastructure. The actions undertaken by Russia, where its cyber operations showed visible overlap with its kinetic activities on the ground, indicate that hybrid warfare was aimed at a swift victory over Ukraine. This strategy, also known as a 'thunder-run', did not succeed for Russia for several reasons, including indecisive strikes due to the Russian need for Ukrainian infrastructure during the invasion. Putin would fear a NATO backlash if the attack transgressed borders, a counter-offensive launched by pro-Ukraine hacktivists, and the lure of conventional attacks overtaking cyber-operations. While there are reports that there were China-affiliated groups targeting Ukrainian digital infrastructure, such instances do not seem to be large-scale, and lack of attribution makes it challenging to substantiate them.

However, on the disinformation front, Russia received more incredible support from China. Russia itself employed disinformation campaigns heavily to create a justification for its actions amongst the masses. One of the major campaigns in this pursuit was neo-Nazi propaganda. The Russian propaganda seems to have succeeded at home in projecting the military operation directed at de-Nazifying Ukraine. The success within Russia appears to stem from tight media control and adept manipulation of facts to concoct a desired narrative. Ukraine's revival of characters and symbols of nationalism that harboured questionable alliances with the Nazis have further added undue credibility to Russian history.

China's role in abetting Russian disinformation is also visible in this conflict. There are several examples where Russian propaganda has been adopted by the Chinese, which can only be described as 'disinformation surrogacy'. This surrogacy pushed Russian propaganda in five ways—assuming disinformation without fact-checks, framing the conflict in favour of Russian interests, suppressing information in contrast to the Russian narrative, invoking whataboutism directed at the USA, and blaming NATO and the USA as the aggressors in the conflict. The first three methods of disinformation surrogacy can be seen as China's gentle way of upholding its 'no limits' commitment. The last two forms of disinformation, the ones targeted at the USA and the NATO can be seen as part of a broader strategy directly aligned with China's own interests. Such narratives paint a picture of grievances similar to Russia's concerning strategic encirclement.

Responding to the dual challenges of cyber-attacks and disinformation campaigns should be treated as a growing priority if sovereign nations like Ukraine are to be defended against bigger states like Russia. A counter-offensive on the cyber front does help limit the adversary's scope of cyber-attacks. Additionally, the onslaught of disinformation also needs to be curbed. After the conflict began, Russia disabled many Western social media platforms to prevent the spread of counter-narratives. Similarly, China has long stopped its citizens' access to unfiltered information from abroad. However, both Russia and China actively carry out disinformation through state-sponsored media and individual official accounts on global social media. This puts both authoritarian states in an advantageous position wherein their narratives can be easily amplified abroad while foreign reports remain restricted at home. In this predicament, a ban on such state-affiliated records concerning an ongoing conflict could be adopted. This would level the playing field with states that do not value freedom of expression. In addition, a rationally thought cyber defence strategy is required to curb such attacks on the fourth front, and permanent support mechanisms should be implemented for smaller nations lacking a robust cyber-security infrastructure.

ENDNOTES

1. P. Polityuk, *"Massive cyberattack hits Ukrainian government websites as West warns on Russia conflict."*, Reuters, January 14, 2022 at https://www.reuters.com/technology/massive-cyberattack-hits-ukrainian-government-websites-amid-russia-tensions-2022-01-14/
2. J. S. Brady, *"Press Briefing by Press Secretary Jen Psaki and FEMA Administrator Deanne Criswell"*, January 14, 2022. Retrieved from White House Press Briefing: https://www.whitehouse.gov/briefing-room/press-briefings/2022/01/14/press-briefing-by-press-secretary-jen-psaki-and-fema-administrator-deanne-criswell-january-14-2022/
3. Centre for Preventive Action, "*Conflict in Ukraine*. Retrieved from CFR: Global Conflict Tracker", May 12, 2022 at https://www.cfr.org/global-conflict-tracker/conflict/conflict-ukraine
4. Vladimirov, Aleksandr Ivanovich. "Obshchey Teorii Voyny. Chast' III." *Gosudarstvo, Voyna i Armiia: Nekotorye Voprosy Teorii* . Moscow: Moscow: Universitet Sinergia Izdatel'skiy Dom, 2018, p. 203.
5. Popov, I. M. and M. Khamzatov. *'Voyna budushchego'*, Brattleboro: Azbuka, 2016.
6. 李炳彦 [Bingyan Li], '"智战时代"与东方兵学智慧' ['"Intelligent Warfare Era" and Eastern Military Science Wisdom'], 孙子研究 [Sun Zi Studies] 16, no. 4 (April 2017): 81–3; 黄志澄 [Zhicheng Huang], '高超声速武器及其对未来战争的影响' ['Hypersonic Weapons and Their Impact on Future Wars'], 1–7.
7. Qiao, Liang and Xiangsui Wang, *'Unrestricted Warfare'*, Echo Point Books, 2015.
8. Saalman, Lora, 'China and its hybrid warfare spectrum', *Hybrid Warfare*. London: Bloomsbury, 2021, pp. 95-112.
9. Dittmer, L., *'China's Continuous Revolution: The Post-Liberation Epoch 1949-1981'*, Berkeley: University of California Press, 1987.
10. P. Jakhar, *"Confucius Institutes: The growth of China's controversial cultural branch"*, BBC, September 07, 2022, at https://www.bbc.com/news/world-asia-china-49511231
11. S. Cook, *"Beijing's Global Megaphone"*, Freedom House, January 2022 at https://freedomhouse.org/sites/default/files/2020-02/01152020_SR_ China_ Global_ Megaphone_with_Recommendations_PDF.pdf
12. J. Tarabay, *"Chinese Hackers Targeted Southeast Asian Nations"*, Bloomberg, December 9, 2022 at https://www.bloomberg.com/news/articles/2021-12-09/chinese-hackers-targeted-southeast-asian-nations-report-says
13. Microsoft, *"Destructive malware targeting Ukrainian organizations"*, Microsoft Security, January 15, 2022, at https://www.microsoft.com/security/blog/2022/01/15/destructive-malware-targeting-ukrainian-organizations/
14. Reuters, *"US, UK: Russia responsible for cyberattack against Ukrainian banks"*, February 19, 2022, at https://www.reuters.com/world/us-says-russia-was-responsible-cyberattack-against-ukrainian-banks-2022-02-18/

15. ESET, *"Ukraine hit by destructive attacks before and during the Russian invasion with HermeticWiper and IsaacWiper"*, ESET Research, March 01, 2022, at https://www.eset.com/int/about/newsroom/press-releases/research/eset-research-ukraine-hit-by-destructive-attacks-before-and-during-the-russian-invasion-with-hermet/
16. J. A. Guerrero-Saade, *"Acid Rain: A Modem Wiper Rains Down on Europe"*, Sentinel Labs, March 31, 2022, at https://www.sentinelone.com/labs/acidrain-a-modem-wiper-rains-down-on-europe/
17. Hayes, Richard E. "Thunder Runs into Baghdad: The Impact of Information Age Command and Control on Conflict." 11th International Command and Control Research and Technology Symposium (ICCRTS): 'Coalition Command and Control in the Networked Era.'. Cambridge: Homeland Security Digital Library, 2006. 26-28.
18. Cattler, D., and Black, D., "The Myth of the Missing Cyberwar", *Foreign Affairs,* April 6, 2022 at The Myth of the Missing Cyberwar | Foreign Affairs
19. Digital Security Unit, *"Ukraine: An overview of Russia's cyberattack activity in Ukraine"*, Microsoft, April 2022, Retrieved from https://query.prod.cms.rt.microsoft.com/cms/api/am/binary/RE4Vwwd
20. Mien, G.S. (n.d.). *"THUNDER RUNS": PANACEA FOR URBAN OPERATION?"*, Ministry of Defence, Singapore, Retrieved April 23, 2022, from https://www.mindef.gov.sg/oms/content/imindef/publications/pointer/supplements/LDAC/_jcr_content/imindefPars/0008/file.res/ThunderRun.pdf
21. M. Starr, *"Ukraine instructs citizens to target Russian supply lines, fuel, food, ammunition"*, *The Jerusalem Post*, March 3, 2022 at https://www.jpost.com/international/article-699200
22. J. Pearson and J. Landay, *"Cyberattack on NATO could trigger collective defence clause - official."*, Reuters, March 1, 2022, at https://www.reuters.com/world/europe/cyberattack-nato-could-trigger-collective-defence-clause-official-2022-02-28/
23. K. Conger and D.E. Sanger, *"Hackers Claim to Target Russian Institutions in Barrage of Cyberattacks and Leaks."*, *The New York Times*, April 22, 2022, at https://www.nytimes.com/2022/04/22/us/politics/hackers-russia-cyberattacks.html
24. Derakhshan, Hossein and Clair Wardle. "Information Disorder: Definitions." *Understanding and Addressing the Disinformation Ecosystem*. Annenberg School for Communications, 2017. 5-12.
25. Fallis, Don, 'The Varieties of Disinformation' in *The Philosophy of Information Quality*, Floridi, Luciano and Phyllis Illari (eds.), Springer, 2014. 135-161.
26. Tzu, Sun. *The art of war*. Chichester: Capstone Publishing, 2010.
27. Huhtinen, A-M and J. Rantapelkonen. "Disinformation in Hybrid Warfare: The Rhizomatic Speed of Social Media in the Spamosphere." *Journal of Information Warfare* (2016): 50-67.
28. Cullen, Patrick J. and Erik Reichborn Kjennerud. "Understanding Hybrid Warfare." 2017.
29. M. Berger, *"Putin says he will 'denazify' Ukraine. Here's the history behind that claim"*, *The Washington Post*, February 26, 2022 at https://www.washingtonpost.com/world/2022/02/24/putin-denazify-ukraine/
30. Esch, Christian. *"Banderites" vs. "New Russia": The Battle Field of History in the Ukraine*

Conflict.", Oxford University Press, 2015. Retrieved from: "Banderites" vs "New Russia", Reuters Institute for the Study of Journalism (ox.ac.uk)

31. Levada Center, *"The Conflict with Ukraine"*, Levada Center, April 11, 2022 at https://www.levada.ru/en/2022/04/11/the-conflict-with-ukraine/
32. Edward Wong and Julian E. Barnes, "China Asked Russia to Delay Ukraine War Until After Olympics, U.S. Officials Say", *The New York Times*, March 2, 2022, at China Asked Russia to Delay Ukraine War Until After Olympics, Biden Officials Say - The New York Times (nytimes.com)
33. China Aerospace Studies Institute. *"Joint Statement of the Russian Federation and the People's Republic of China on the International Relations Entering a New Era and the Global Sustainable Development"*, China Aerospace Studies Institute, February 4, 2022, at https://www.airuniversity.af.edu/Portals/10/CASI/documents/Translations/2022-02-04%20China%20Russia%20joint%20statement%20International%20 Relations%20Entering%20a%20New%20Era.pdf
34. A. Teraoka, *"Chinese hackers launch cyberattacks against Ukraine amid war"*, Nikkei Asia, April 7, 202, at https://asia.nikkei.com/Politics/Ukraine-war/Chinese-hackers-launch-cyberattacks-against-Ukraine-amid-war
35. L. Yuan, *"How China Embraces Russian Propaganda and Its Version of the War"*, *The New York Times*, March 4, 2022 at https://www.nytimes.com/2022/03/04/business/china-russia-ukraine-disinformation.html
36. Politico, *"Videos show that Ukraine President Volodymyr Zelenskyy uses cocaine"*, Politifact, April 23, 2022, at https://www.politifact.com/factchecks/2022/apr/26/facebook-posts/viral-videos-falsely-claiming-ukraines-zelenskyy-u/
37. US-China Perception Monitor, *"Chinese Public Opinion on the War in Ukraine"*, April 19, 2022, at https://uscnpm.org/2022/04/19/chinese-public-opinion-war-in-ukraine/
38. A. Gabuev and L. Kovachich, "Comrades in Tweets? The Contours and Limits of China-Russia Cooperation on Digital Propaganda" *The Moscow Times*, June 3, 2021, at https://www.themoscowtimes.com/2021/06/03/comrades-in-tweets-the-contours-and-limits-of-china-russia-cooperation-on-digital-propaganda-a74099
39. Z. Cooper, B. Schafer and E. Soula, *"China's State Media and Government Officials Are Backing Russia on Ukraine"*, Alliance for Securing Democracy, March 13, 2022, at https://securingdemocracy.gmfus.org/chinas-state-media-and-government-officials-are-backing-russia-on-ukraine-war/
40. Reuters, *"China's foreign minister speaks with Ukrainian counterpart"*, April 5, 2022, at https://www.reuters.com/world/chinas-foreign-minister-speaks-with-ukrainian-counterpart-2022-04-05/
41. Xin, Liu [@LiuXininBeijing]. "Can you help me fight your friend so that I can concentrate on fighting you later?", Twitter, March 19, 2022, https://twitter.com/LiuXininBeijing/status/1505043155682402306?s=20&t=Bm71mqX2d9225ZXmsVkbh
42. S. Cook, *"The CCP's Ukraine War Propaganda"*, *The Diplomat*, April 16, 2022, at https://thediplomat.com/2022/04/the-ccps-ukraine-war-propaganda/
43. Dykstra, A, 'The Rhetoric of "Whataboutism" in American Journalism and Political Identity', *Res Rhetorica*, 2020, pp. 2-16. doi:10.29107/rr2020.2.1.
44. Z. Cooper, B. Schafer and E. Soula, *"China's State Media and Government Officials*

Are Backing Russia on Ukraine", Alliance for Securing Democracy, March 13, 2022, at https://securingdemocracy.gmfus.org/chinas-state-media-and-government-officials-are-backing-russia-on-ukraine-war/

45. M. Koetse, *"How Chinese State Media's 'America is Bad' Hashtags Are Backfiring on Weibo"*, What's on Weibo, April 16, 2022, at https://www.whatsonweibo.com/how-chinese-state-medias-america-is-bad-hashtags-are-backfiring-on-weibo/
46. Zhong Sheng (*People's Daily*), *"U.S. has inescapable responsibilities for Ukraine crisis"*, People's Daily Online, March 30, 2022 at http://en.people.cn/n3/2022/0330/c90000-10077602.html

CHAPTER 8

Russia-China Axis and the Cold War 2.0

Sukanya Bali

ABSTRACT

Russia's invasion of Ukraine has put the world in a dilemma with the possibility of a new Cold War scenario. China has been trying to stay neutral to secure its relationship with Russia and Ukraine. This chapter examines the three essential dynamics considering China's bilateral relations with both. First, what is China's posture in the Russia-Ukraine crisis amid its strong relationship with Moscow? China refused to condemn the invasion in the early days and called upon the West to address Moscow's legitimate concerns. Beijing also refers to Russia's invasion as "a special military operation" and "the Russia-Ukraine crisis". Second, what are the contours of Beijing-Moscow and Beijing-Ukraine relations? This chapter will look closely at it from an economic, social, technological, and political angle, with China being the largest trading partner of both Russia and Ukraine. Both countries are part of China's ambitious Belt and Road Initiative, which came in 2013. Lastly, a Cold War approach seems looming amid the war in the international scenario between the Western countries and the Russia-China axis. Governments seem to be aligning into blocs reminiscent of the Cold War era. What are the implications of such a China-Russia axis for the future of European security and international relations? In Cold War 2.0, China's growth may rise as a looming threat in the 21st century with a fear of new poles of power being redefined. The research relies on primary and secondary data collection methods.

Key words: *China-Russia, China-Ukraine, BRI, Cold War.*

Introduction

This chapter seeks to lighten the changing dynamics among the three major countries, i.e., China, Russia, and Ukraine, amid the current Russia-Ukraine crisis and how other nations react to it. The war has now been prolonged for over 100-days, with no end in sight. Ukraine continues to fight for its sovereignty as Moscow pursues its expansionist approach. Russia's invasion has raised speculation among countries and has increased monitoring of its potential move to counterbalance Moscow's offensive and bring back stability in the region. President Vladimir Putin, in his statements, continues to assert Ukraine as an "illegitimate country exists on land that's historically and rightfully Russian".[1]

Contours of Russia-Ukraine Relations

In 1991, Ukraine voted for independence; since then, it has struggled to come out of Russia's shadow. Ukraine joined the North Atlantic Treaty Organization's (NATO) Partnership for peace along with Russia in 1994. Russia remained a member of the peace partnership until 2014, when NATO suspended the ties. In 1996, a few countries signed the Budapest Memorandum on Security Assurances, following Ukraine's accession to NPT as a non-nuclear state. Signatories Russia, the United Kingdom (UK), and the United States of America (USA) assured and respected Kyiv's decision to maintain sovereignty, territorial integrity, and independence.

Ukraine's former president, Leonid Kuchma, met NATO leaders in July 1997 to establish a partnership with the defence alliance and agreed to engage twice a year to strengthen the relationship. Soon after, Moscow blocked gas supply through Ukraine, which accounts for 80 per cent of its export to Europe. The shutdown hit Kyiv's economy and dented political stability. Russia, since the beginning, protested against Ukraine's membership in NATO, claiming it is "not even a real nation-state".[2] The Ukrainian-speaking population in the West pushed for closer ties with Europe, while Russian speakers in the east pushed for more significant links with Russia. In 2014, pro-Russian president Victor Yanukovych who sought to build closer ties with Moscow fled Kyiv amid mounting opposition to his rule. His successor tried to draw the country closer to the West.

In 2014, President Yanukovych declined to join a closer relationship with the EU, sparking protests known as Euromaidan across the country. The protests forced the pro-Russian leaders out of power. Putin called it a fascist coup that threatened the lives of Russian speakers in Crimea and ordered its invasion. In March 2014, Putin decried that a western partner had crossed the line in Ukraine. Russia moved in troops, held a controversial referendum, and annexed Crimea.[3] The Soviet Union gave Crimea to Ukraine in 1954 to strengthen ties between the countries.

Russia also armed separatists in the Donbas region, and the Kremlin carved a pro-Russia buffer zone in Western Ukraine that provides a means to pressure and undermine the European ambitions of Kyiv. Russia referred to the region with most ethnic Russians as New Russia and extended material support to secessionist movements. Moscow justifies its incursions in Ukraine to protect the interests of the 8 million Russian Diasporas in Ukraine. Russian familial bonds in Ukraine date back centuries. The historical and cultural significance of Kyiv, sometimes referred to as the 'mother of all Russia,' makes it imperative to have Ukraine under the Russian sphere of influence.

Economically, Russia depended on pipelines in Ukraine to supply its gas to east European countries and gave billions of dollars in transit fees. The supply continued in 2022 despite rising tensions. Until recent years, Russia was Ukraine's largest trading partner, and Moscow had tried to draw Kyiv into its Eurasian Economic Union.

A westernized Ukraine aligned to the strategic priorities of the West is an abomination for Putin's Russia. Putin's worldview had long emphasized unity among eastern Slavs—Russians, Ukrainians, and Belarusians—and believed that Russia, Ukraine, and Belarus should aspire for a common political destiny. Besides, Russia also has clear cultural, economic, and political bonds and aspirations central to Russia's identity.

In 2021, Putin reiterated his views on Ukraine in an article about the shared heritage of Ukraine and Russia.[4] The European Union and NATO's push eastward towards Ukraine was unacceptable to Putin. Russia has consistently prevented Ukraine from drifting to the Western sphere of influence. Despite Moscow's opposition, Ukraine built its partnership with NATO and aspired to full membership. It held joint exercises and became an opportunity partner of NATO in 2020, espousing a special status as the bloc's non-member ally.

In the weeks ahead of Russia's invasion, Putin made several demands to alter the European Union's security architecture. Russia wanted a security architecture more conducive to Russian security interests. Russia demanded that NATO stop expanding toward its borders and seek

Moscow's approval for specific NATO deployments. Putin hoped that the West would cease supporting the promotion of Western-style democracy in Ukraine and elsewhere that could undermine his regime. However, the Western alliance turned down Putin's demands.

For a year, Russia had been amassing troops and war machinery on the Ukrainian border under the pretext of military exercises. In February 2022, Putin ordered a full-scale attack on Ukraine as part of a special military operation to demilitarize and de-nazify Ukraine and depose the government. The invasion witnessed strong opposition by the Ukrainians and inflicted heavy casualties on either side. By May 2022, Russian troops had focused their attacks on the eastern parts of Ukraine. The port city of Mariupol fell to Russian forces and they are on the brink of taking Severodonetsk, the last large city to be brought under their control in the province of Luhansk.

China and Russia's rapprochement

Beijing and Moscow share a long history of security, diplomatic cooperation, and ideological alignment. However, they drifted apart in the 1950s amid disagreements over the development of communism, and tension rose in the 1960s during the border conflict. The relationship was restored with the 2001 Sino-Soviet border agreement. The agreement sought to address border issues and identified areas of cooperation from economics and trade to counterterrorism. The border treaty was renewed in July 2021 for five more years.

Under the current leadership of Chinese President Xi Jinping and Russian President Vladimir Putin, the partnership has showcased a growth in mutual trust. Xi claimed the concept of Sino-Russia relations established by the treaty is a "generational friendship" and is "in line with the fundamental interests of both countries". Xi also emphasized that it is "consistent with the theme of a peace era" to build new relations and a "community of common identity". Both the leaders have met several times and underscored the importance of their partnership. Recently, Chinese Foreign Ministry spokesperson Zhao Lijian said, "An important takeaway from the success of China-Russia relations is that the two sides rise above the model of military and political alliance in the Cold War era." He added that they "commit themselves to develop a new international relations model".[5]

Russia's dependency on China has increased since the outbreak of the pandemic. A wide range of areas of cooperation has held the two most considerable Eurasian powers together. Moreover, EU-USA sanctions on Russia since 2014 have pushed Moscow closer to Beijing's economic clout. Trade turnover between the countries increased over the years, and Russia's central bank raised the Chinese Yuan proportion in foreign reserves from 0.1 per cent in 2015 to 13.2 per cent in 2020. The China-Russia partnership can be assessed for its political, economic, military, and technological cooperation to understand the depth of the relationship.

Politically, China and Russia cross-border relations have grown. In 2019, China and Russia announced a "Comprehensive Strategic Partnership of Coordination for a New Era", which aimed at "professing a high degree of political trust and all-around cooperation".[6] Later, in 2021, both sides signed a "Road Map for Military Co-operation for 2021-2025"[7] and founded the Eurasia-based Shanghai Cooperation Organization (SCO) to focus on security affairs.[8] Decades of ideological rift took a back seat in the global order dominated by Western democracies. The nature of the political regimes and the political values of the ruling elite are similar, and their economies complement each other. They have adopted similar approaches on issues like human rights and the internet, and both are wary of the influence of Western democracies.

Economically, the Carnegie Moscow Centre reported that Beijing's share in Moscow trade increased from 10.5 per cent, i.e., USD 88.8 billion, in 2013 to 15.7 per cent, USD 108.3 billion in 2019.[9] China's exports to Russia account for over 70 per cent of the oil of Moscow's exports. In 2019, Russia overtook Saudi Arabia as the top supplier to China. Since COVID-19, the trade turnover reached a high of 17.3 per cent. The deepening of the Sino-Russia partnership went far beyond trade. In 2010, the China Development Bank loaned Russia's state-owned company, Rosneft, around USD 15 billion to complete the construction of the Eastern Siberia–Pacific Ocean (ESPO) branch oil pipeline from Skovorodino-Mohe[10] (further from the Chinese border town of Mohe to Daqing) which will additionally provide Russian crude oil for 25 years. Beijing remains the major buyer of Moscow's coal and metal in the region. On the other hand, Moscow depends heavily on Beijing's capital, goods, and services.

Russia became a practical alternative after the collapse of the Soviet

Union in 1991, with most of the PRC's designing and building of modern weapons coming from the technology, reams of technical data and consultation from Russian engineers. Militarily, while China has shifted some of its manufacturing to the domestic market, most of its weaponry still comes from Moscow. According to the Stockholm International Peace Research Institute (SIPRI), Beijing's imported arms account for more than 77 per cent from 2016 to 2020, making China the second-largest arms recipient from Russia.[11] In 2018, Russia's military forces completed the most significant military exercise in which 3,200 Chinese People's Liberation Army soldiers joined. In 2019, Putin announced, "Moscow is helping Beijing create its missile early warning system, thus tying China's strategic nuclear deterrent to a Russian technological backbone".[12]

Technologically, Military-technical and space cooperation had existed but gained speed in recent years with Moscow agreeing to supply Su-35 fighter jets and S-499 defence systems. The two countries decided to develop an international scientific lunar station in the space arena and have adopted a joint position toward a USA-led space order. In 2019, Russia imported USD 30.8 billion worth of technology-related equipment products from China.[13]

In recent years, Chinese technology and firms such as Huawei have made significant inroads in Russian markets. With the enhanced cooperation on 5G, robotics and digital economy, and information and communication technology, countries have initiated several forums to facilitate collaboration in science and technology, including setting up a Russia-China venture fund and Russia-China innovation dialogue. The countries wish to encourage talent exchanges and believe that China's industrial applications and Moscow's research and talent can add value to each other's science and technology aspirations

The relationship between Beijing and Moscow, after a tumultuous past, grew stronger in several areas amid the greater competition with the West. Besides the areas of cooperation, the countries began expressing their relationship through the rhetoric of friendship between leaders in the years leading up to the Ukraine-Russia conflict. They pledged cooperation, adopted an identical approach to global issues, and pushed for a new world order. Xi Jinping called Putin his closest friend while the countries locked horns with the West. The alignment of global strategic ambitions drew the nations together. In the early days of the outbreak of the Russia-Ukraine conflict, China refused to condemn the invasion and called upon the West to address Moscow's legitimate concerns.

Beijing referred to Russia's invasion as "a special military operation" and "the Russia-Ukraine crisis".[14] Although Beijing seems flexible, it calls its relationship to "form partnerships, not alliances". Where everyone seems apart, the current status clears Russia's isolation following its invasion and has made Beijing a close partner. Zhao Lijian further reiterated that China "maintains that the sovereignty and territorial integrity of all countries should be respected and safeguarded" and that "Ukraine's sovereignty and security should be preserved, and Russia's legitimate security concerns should also be respected".[15]

With a familiar posture, Beijing and Moscow have raised the same common threat perception from the West. They have aligned their "core interest of upholding international equity and justice" against the USA's "unilateralism". The PRC and Russia's relationship resembles a non-binding alignment based on opposing the USA-led world order and "de-dollarize" the global economy. Both nations feel the need to put an end to "external interference and regional security threats" posed by liberal democracy partnerships.[16] The increased momentum in the Sino-Russia relationship indicates a renewed interest in common strategic ambitions in a world dominated by Western liberal agenda.

Soon after the Russian invasion, after the Winter Olympics, a joint statement by the Chinese leader expressed support for Moscow's idea to create 'long-term legally binding security guarantees in Europe' and emphasized that the new inter-state relationship between the countries is more profound than the alliances of the Cold War. The statement also expressed opposition to external forces undermining security and stability in the common adjacent regions of the two countries. It is unclear whether the Chinese leader was aware of Russia's plan of action in Ukraine, but China has walked a tightrope between the West and Russia since the invasion.

Putin unveiled new Russian gas deals with Beijing worth an estimated USD 117.5 billion and promised to ramp up Russia's Far East exports at a time of heightened tension with European customers over Ukraine. A new contract to supply 10 billion cubic metres (bcm) of gas per year to China for 25 years from Russia's Far East was also signed. A few days after the outbreak of hostilities in Ukraine, Russia's Gazprom announced to perform a survey of the gas pipeline that planned to deliver up to 50 bcm of Russian gas to China.

Moscow has sent gas to China via its Power of Siberia pipeline since 2019 by shipping LNG. It exported 16.5 bcm of gas to China in 2021, including 10.5 bcm via the Power of Siberia, which is separate from the pipelines that send gas to Europe.[17] Beijing is committed to purchase additional natural gas from Russia. In March, Wang Yi, Chinese Foreign Minister, asserted, "No matter how perilous and challenging the international situation may be, China and Russia will maintain their strategic focus and steadily advance comprehensive strategic partnership of coordination for the new era".[18]

These energy deals and the optics of Putin's visit to China ahead of the invasion indicate strong bilateral relationships across political and economic spheres. They also show the urge the countries share to challenge the existing world order. Both nations seek to imply joint approaches to international concerns of human rights and the internet in a USA-centric world. However, it is unlikely that President Xi would throw China's weight around to support Putin with the strategic and security priorities in Ukraine and beyond and draw the anger of the global community.

China and Ukraine surging relations

Ukraine had built strong relations and cooperation with China in the military-technical and space domain. Both the countries established diplomatic ties in 1992; since then, many strategic partnerships have been signed. In 2011, a Joint Declaration on the establishment and development of a strategic partnership was followed by the Treaty on Friendship and Cooperation Between China and Ukraine in 2013. The Chinese supported Kyiv's efforts and aimed "to protect the unity and territorial integrity of Ukraine".[19] Beijing also assured "unconditionally not to use or threaten to use nuclear weapons against Ukraine as a non-nuclear-weapon state and to provide corresponding security assurances to Ukraine in the event of aggression or threat of aggression against Ukraine using nuclear weapons".

Beijing and Kyiv's relations amid political chaos, economic upliftment, and technological exchange have undergone diverse dynamics. The relationship gradually changed after 2014; after the armed aggression of

Russia, Ukraine chose: to integrate into the EU and NATO to ensure its economic and military security. Recently, the ties between the two have improved.

Politically, Ukraine positioned itself as China's key access point for entering the European market. Soon after coming to power, Ukrainian President Volodymyr Zelenskyy, in a telephonic conversation with President Xi, called Beijing "Ukraine's no. 1 trade and economic partner in the world" and hoped Ukraine becomes "a bridge to Europe for Chinese business".[20] In June 2021, Kyiv also withdrew from a joint statement issued for an independent investigation into human rights abuses in the Xinjiang region by more than forty countries.[21]

Economically, Beijing supported Ukraine in various infrastructural development projects. In 2016, Beijing built a terminal at Mykolaiv port on the Black Sea for easy transfer of grain and oil. In 2017, Ukraine joined China's BRI, which aims to recuperate the infrastructure and modify transport via the road and rail sector. Both nations signed construction contracts worth USD 3 billion in the transportation and energy industry.

In 2013, China's Xinjiang Construction and Production Corps signed an agreement with Ukraine's KSG Agro Company to lease 100,000 agricultural lands for over 50 years. In 2017, China also completed the Ukraine international port, Yuzhny, near Odessa. Beijing's National Building Material Company constructed more than 10 solar power plants, accounting for half of the installed solar power capacity in the country. More than 6,000 Chinese nationals are working on ongoing projects.

Kyiv increased revenue from oil and gas reserves with Xinjiang Beiken Energy Engineering, a Beijing firm. A Chinese firm built a subway line worth USD 1.3 billion in the capital. Since 2020, China has become Ukraine's top trading partner. Kyiv exported USD 7.26 billion of products such as iron ore, corn, and seed oils. With the growing trade, Kyiv overtook the USA as Beijing's largest corn supplier. In the last 25 years, exports to Beijing have increased by 12.2 per cent. In 2020, the trade turnover between the countries was USD 15.4 billion. Ukraine is also a critical entrepôt for China's Belt and Road Initiative ambitions.[22]

Militarily, both countries share a strong partnership in exchanging military equipment. In 1998, Beijing purchased its first aircraft carrier,

Varyag, from Ukraine, later upgraded by the PLA navy as *Liaoning*. Soon after the post-Tiananmen arms embargo, Beijing turned to many partner nations for supplying military technologies and equipment for the PLA Navy and Air Force. As seen in Figure 8.1 below, according to SIPRI, from 2016 to 2020, Ukraine accounted for 6.3 per cent, i.e., USD 80-90 million of arms supply to Beijing. Further, Ukraine has also partnered in building various aircraft carriers, such as Bison air-cushioned landing craft, which help in landing operations on the islands in the East and the South China Sea.[23]

Figure 8.1: Ukraine's arms supply to Beijing: 1990-2020

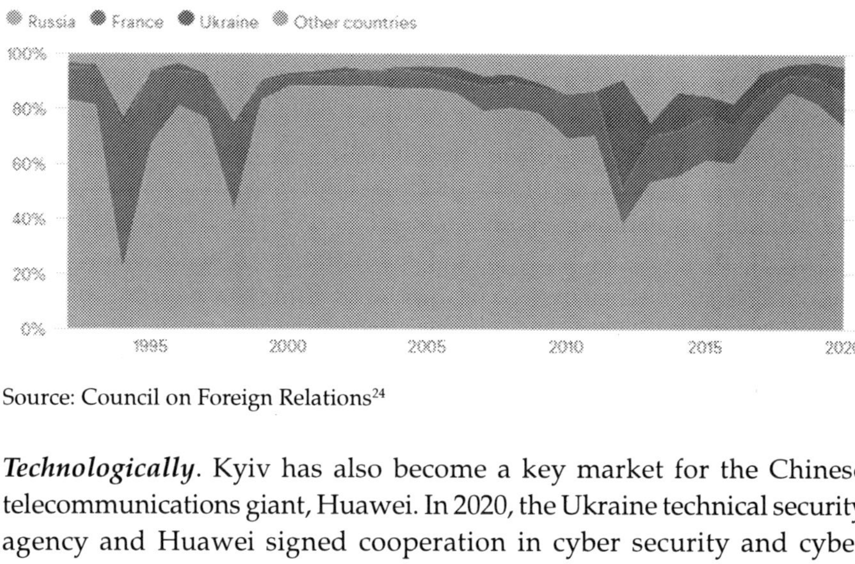

Source: Council on Foreign Relations[24]

Technologically. Kyiv has also become a key market for the Chinese telecommunications giant, Huawei. In 2020, the Ukraine technical security agency and Huawei signed cooperation in cyber security and cyber defence systems. Chinese companies seek opportunities in Ukraine's energy sector, including its renewables (solar and wind) and nuclear power. Kyiv hopes to attain self-sufficiency in uranium and has been discussing investments with the China Development Bank. Further, Beijing seeks to strengthen its uranium production in Ukraine to secure China's uranium supplies.

Rising Cold War 2.0?

The world has been rapidly changing to a more expansionist and alliance-based order. Nations have become more national-interest centric. The changing global leadership to a China-centric world is a far-fetched idea, but what remains common is the USA in the new Cold War. A new scenario of the West with Europe and China with Russia has gained light. The Biden Administration is focused on persuading its allies, Europe in particular, on forming a united front against Russia. The Russia-Ukraine war has brought Cold War dynamics into international relations. Countries across the globe picked sides in the war, consolidating alliances in blocs reminiscent of the post-World War II era.

Cold War debates and narratives of containing Russia emerged among defence and security strategists in the West. Tensions increased in the post-Cold War security architecture of Europe. All these developments, amid international rivalry between the West and China, have deepened the partnership between Moscow and Beijing, posturing the Russia-China axis on one side and the transatlantic relationship led by the USA on the other.

Scholars invoked a reference to the Cold War, with officials of governments and international organizations in their narratives to describe the severity of the crisis since the outbreak of the conflict. Many leaders and commentators analyze the current situation taking the Cold War as the benchmark. James Hersberg, a professor at GWU, said the Ukraine crisis is squarely a "cold war echo".[25] Professor Fredrik Logevall at Harvard says, "If we mean a titanic struggle that involves all aspects of national power waged between two incompatible systems but short of outright military conflict—then yeah, I guess this is a cold war". The UN General-Secretary warned that miscommunication between global powers could be disastrous and that the world is "more dangerous than during the Cold War."[26]

The Ukraine crisis has quickly brought back the Cold War mentality in the narrative built around Washington. President Biden said they would save democracies. The war renewed and strengthened the transatlantic alliances and put the old Cold War machinery into action against Russia. Interestingly, the crisis pushed Western disunity and brought allied countries together to fight a common enemy. Many multinational companies have partially or entirely shut down operations in Russia, some of which had been operating since the Cold War. Pepsi, McDonald's, GM, and Coke have scaled down or shut operations in Russia to protest against the Russian invasion. Some ventures like Burger King have redirected their profits from Russia for relief operations in Ukraine. The West-aligned corporations have followed the transatlantic plan to sever ties with Russia. The 'us' vs 'them' rhetoric has gained momentum since the invasion.

Like in the Cold War, the West-allied countries agreed to buy and send weapons to a war zone and support Ukraine. They sanctioned Russian officials and oligarchs, banned Russian institutions from the SWIFT financial system, and affected their ability to function globally. The Europeans have also closed the air space to Russian planes and seized assets like the multi-million-dollar yachts of people with close ties to Putin. This concerted action against Russia reverberates with the echoes of the Cold War.

Hawks in the USA are pushing for a two-front Cold War against Russia and China. The Russia-China rapprochement in recent years and close friendship between the leaders has caused the Western allied countries to view their axis as a bloc against their common interests. So far, China has maintained a neutral stand and refrained from voicing support for Russia's actions in Ukraine. China has highlighted three issues for the Russian invasion, namely, NATO's expansion, the EU's expansion, and US unilateralism, which might portray Beijing as in line with Moscow's interests. However, it is unclear at this stage if China would extend support to Russia's invasion and draw the ire of the Western coalition. China has been trying to maintain a positive relationship with the EU, but the crisis has inclined the EU towards the USA. This shifting and alignment of interests signal the brewing of a Cold War era, and it seems no matter how the invasion ends, a new Cold War appears inevitable.

Putin's perception of the invasion and the European security architecture

For Putin, the end of the Cold War with the disintegration of the Soviet Union was the biggest catastrophe of the 21st century. The breakdown of the USSR is remembered as a time of humiliation in Russian circles of power. Putin believes the Ukrainians and Russians comprise one people, and their shared history implies they have a common destiny. He elaborates on the theme in his article published in 2021.[27] Putin laments the humiliation of the Soviet Union and Ukraine's independence with the end of the Cold War and explains partly his priority to prevent Ukraine from drifting closer to the West. Putin blames NATO and the EU for stoking identity politics to create an 'anti-Moscow Russia' in Ukraine and reiterated the same in the speech before launching the special military operation. Kremlin's launching of the attack on Ukraine is giving rise to a Cold War scenario with stakeholders having conflicting aspirations towards European security and Ukraine's independence.

The Russian President has sought to undo the European security framework that was created after the downfall of the Soviet Union and has set off to recreate a historical buffer zone. He has strongly expressed that he is prepared to accomplish this not just by diplomatic means but also by using force. For Putin, the fight to roll back his country's defeat in the Cold War has already lasted at least 15 years.

The end of the Cold War defined the European security architecture. Ukraine was allied with the USA and emerged as a strategic partner. In 1994, the country agreed in the Budapest memorandum to forgo nuclear arms left by the Russians in return for assurances from the USA, Britain, and Russia to respect its security and sovereignty. Ukraine and other Soviet satellite states aspired to join Western groupings like NATO and the EU. In 2008, Russia had made it clear that NATO membership of Ukraine and Georgia would be a redline. Putin emphasized that granting NATO membership to the duo would be a direct threat to Moscow. However, the West tried to expand eastward through NATO and the EU, gradually upsetting the security framework that maintained peace in Europe. In 2007, Putin declared his rejection of the America-led world order at the Munich Security Conference and warned of "unexploded ordnance" left behind from the Cold War: "ideological stereotypes" and "double standards" that allowed Washington to rule the world while crimping Russia's development.

In 2014, the USA overthrew a democratically elected pro-Russia president of Ukraine. Later in February, Russian forces took over Crimea and were stirred by separatists in eastern Ukraine. John Mearsheimer argues that the West should be blamed for the Ukraine crisis. In 2014, he said that Putin's actions in Ukraine align with the realist interpretation of international politics. Given that France during Napoleon, imperial Germany, and Nazi Germany crossed Ukraine to strike Russia adds a lot of strategic value to Ukraine as a buffer state, and hence Kyiv going under the influence of the West is unacceptable to Russia's strategic thinking. In the current crisis, Putin has again drawn Washington's attention to respect Russia's concerns in its backyard. The USA and the West is supporting Ukraine through arms, intelligence etc. and aiding an overt involvement in the confrontation with Russia.

John Mearsheimer, a critic of the USA's foreign policy, argues that the current crisis is the fault of the USA and the Western alliances. He blames them for disregarding Russia's security concerns in the European security architecture. He states, "If you live in a world where there are three great powers—China, Russia, and the United States—and one of those great powers, China, is a peer competitor, what you want to do if you're the United States—is have Russia on your side of the ledger. Instead, what we have done with our foolish policies in Eastern Europe is drive the Russians into the arms of the Chinese. This is a violation of Balance of Power Politics."[28]

Conclusion

The Russia-Ukraine war has startled the economies and raised speculations and various considerations across the globe. Oil prices have risen to the highest since 2008, the European security architecture has undergone strains not seen since the Cold War, and a formation of a Russian-China axis loomed large. With the growing intensity of war due to the Russian expansion, the Ukrainians are paying the horrendous price with their lives and heritage. The miscalculation of Russia has already exacerbated the war situation, and the Western alliance led by the USA extended support to Ukrainians and mounted sanctions against Russia. A Cold War-like scenario developed in the international community with the Western associations on one end and the Russia-China axis on the other.

However, for China, collaboration with Russia has become a reputational risk that could threaten its economic ambition and strategic priorities. By and large, Xi has tried to indicate that he stands with Russia with "no limits" on friendship. Still, it looks unlikely that Beijing would risk secondary sanctions and its strategic ambitions in Asia to support Moscow. Additionally, once the war ends, China might struggle to rebuild its relationship with Ukraine.

The Russia-Ukraine scenario also raised regional security and peace concerns in the European security architecture. Whatever the war's outcome, Europe's security and deterrence with reference to Russia would undergo significant changes. Moscow has primarily challenged the stability of Europe, which might leave revisionist Russia once again in isolation. The sanctions might leave its economy and society crippled, further weakening Putin's Russia globally.

Moreover, the war has also shifted the security strategy across the Nordic region. Sweden and Finland have already applied for NATO membership. Recently, a majority of 65.8 per cent of voters in Denmark voted in favour of adopting the EU defence and security policy. Interestingly, the war is drawing many European countries away from their long-drawn reluctance to align with the alliance-led European security. Additionally, NATO's continued expansion might stir further Russian aggression and raise uncertainty in the Eurasian region.

The paradigm of international politics shifted after the COVID-19 outbreak, with many powers trying to come forward to give solutions and become an alternative to China. However, clearly, China has emerged stronger after the pandemic than other countries. Amid the war, smaller countries will continue to align themselves with one of the major powers in the neighbourhood to ensure its security, sovereignty and survival, essentially dividing the world into blocs. Consequently, we see a structural shift in the relationship between countries amid the war, and the dependency on the more extraordinary powers like the USA and China will likely prevail worldwide.

ENDNOTES

1. Jade McGlynn, "Russia's Imperial Arrogance Is Destroying Ukrainian Heritage", *Foreign Policy*, 30 May 2022 at https://foreignpolicy.com/2022/05/30/russias-imperial-arrogance-is-destroying-ukrainian-heritage/.
2. "Ukraine's Struggle for Independence in Russia's Shadow", Council on Foreign Relations, at https://www.cfr.org/timeline/ukraines-struggle-independence-russias-shadow.
3. "The China-Ukraine Partnership: Surviving a Deteriorating Strategic Environment", Institut Montaigne, 09 February 2022 at https://www.institutmontaigne.org/en/blog/china-ukraine-partnership-surviving-deteriorating-strategic-environment.
4. Article by Vladimir Putin "On the Historical Unity of Russians and Ukrainians", President of Russia, 12 July 2021 at http://en.kremlin.ru/events/president/news/66181 .
5 "China Calls Russia Relationship a 'New Model' for the World", *Times*, 29 April 2022 at https://time.com/6172135/china-russia-relationship/
6. "Xi Jinping Meets with President Vladimir Putin of Russia", Ministry of Foreign Affairs of the People's Republic of China, 18 November, 2019 at https://www.fmprc.gov.cn/ce/cgmb/eng/zgyw/t1716588.htm
7. Jon Grevatt , "China, Russia approve 2021–25 road map to increase military co-

operation", *Jane's*, 24 November, 2021 at https://www.janes.com/defence-news/news-detail/china-russia-approve-202125-road-map-to-increase-military-co-operation
8. "Report to Congress on the Relationship Between China and Russia", USNI news, 20 May 2022 at https://news.usni.org/2022/05/20/report-to-congress-on-the-relationship-between-china-and-russia
9. Alexander Gabuev and Temur Umarov, "Will the Pandemic Increase Russia's Economic Dependence on China?", Carnegie Endowment for International Peace, 08 July 2020 at https://carnegiemoscow.org/2020/07/08/will-pandemic-increase-russia-s-economic-dependence-on-china-pub-81893
10. "FACTBOX-Russia's ESPO oil pipeline link to China", Reuters, 27 September 2010 at https://www.reuters.com/article/russia-china-pipeline-idUKTOE68Q04I20100927
11. Maryann Xue, "China's arms trade: which countries does it buy from and sell to?" *South China Morning Post*, 04 July 2021 at https://www.scmp.com/news/china/military/article/3139603/how-china-grew-buyer-major-arms-trade-player
12. Alexander Gabuev and Temur Umarov, "Will the Pandemic Increase Russia's Economic Dependence on China?" Carnegie Endowment for International Peace, 08 July 2020 at https://carnegiemoscow.org/2020/07/08/will-pandemic-increase-russia-s-economic-dependence-on-china-pub-81893
13. Ibid.
14. "Russian Federation Announces 'Special Military Operation' in Ukraine as Security Council Meets in Eleventh-Hour Effort to Avoid Full-Scale Conflict", United Nations, 23 February 2022 at https://www.un.org/press/en/2022/sc14803.doc.htm
15. "Wang Yi Expounds China's Five-Point Position on the Current Ukraine Issue", Ministry of Foreign Affairs of Peoples Republic of China, 26 February 2022 at https://www.fmprc.gov.cn/eng/zxxx_662805/202202/t20220226_10645855.html#:~:text=China%20maintains%20that%20the%20sovereignty,abided%20by%20in%20real%20earnest
16. Nirupama Subramanian, "Explained: The China-Russia relationship", *The Indian Express*, 10 February 2022 at https://indianexpress.com/article/explained/explained-the-china-russia-relationship-ukraine-putin-xi-jingping-7763398/
17. Chen Aizhu, "Russia, China agree 30-year gas deal via new pipeline, to settle in euros", Reuters, 04 February 2022 at https://www.reuters.com/world/asia-pacific/exclusive-russia-china-agree-30-year-gas-deal-using-new-pipeline-source-2022-02-04/
18. "State Councillor and Foreign Minister Wang Yi Meets the Press", Ministry of Foreign Affairs of People's Republic of China, 07 March 2022 at https://www.fmprc.gov.cn/eng/zxxx_662805/202203/t20220308_10649559.html
19. Kawashima Shin, "China and the War in Ukraine: Anatomy of a Tightrope Act", Nippon, 26 April 2022 at https://www.nippon.com/en/in-depth/a08101/
20. "Zelensky, Chinese President Xi Jinping hold first telephone conversation", *Kyiv Post*, 13 July 2021 at https://www.kyivpost.com/ukraine-politics/zelensky-chinese-president-xi-jinping-hold-first-telephone-conversation.html
21. Zongyuan Zoe Liu, "What's at Stake for China's Economic Relationship With Ukraine?" Council on Foreign Relations, 02 March 2022 at https://www.cfr.org/in-brief/whats-stake-chinas-economic-relationship-ukraine

22. Elizabeth Wishnick, "Ukraine: China's Burning Bridge to Europe?", *The Diplomat*, 02 February 2022 at https://thediplomat.com/2022/02/ukraine-chinas-burning-bridge-to-europe/
23. "Global arms trade falls slightly, but imports to Europe, East Asia and Oceania rise", Stockholm International Peace Research Institute, 14 March 2022 at https://www.sipri.org/media/press-release/2022/global-arms-trade-falls-slightly-imports-europe-east-asia-and-oceania-rise
24. Zongyuan Zoe Liu, "What's at Stake for China's Economic Relationship With Ukraine?" Council on Foreign Relations, 02 March 2022 at https://www.cfr.org/in-brief/whats-stake-chinas-economic-relationship-ukraine
25. Jake Coyle, "In Russian invasion of Ukraine, Cold War echoes reverberate", Associated Press, 17 March 2022 at https://apnews.com/article/cold-war-echoes-russia-us-ukraine-0050dd806e5f8748bf59b5e84d15b959
26. Karl Ritter, "UN chief: Security threat seems higher than during Cold War", Associated Press, 18 February 2022 at https://apnews.com/article/russia-ukraine-germany-united-nations-soviet-union-europe-76989058442a66048d1993b3cff03d50
27. Article by Vladimir Putin "On the Historical Unity of Russians and Ukrainians", President of Russia, 12 July 2021 at http://en.kremlin.ru/events/president/news/66181
28. Isaac Chotiner, "Why John Mearsheimer Blames the U.S. for the Crisis in Ukraine", *The New Yorker*, 01 March, 2022 at https://www.newyorker.com/news/q-and-a/why-john-mearsheimer-blames-the-us-for-the-crisis-in-ukraine

Annexure 1: North Korea's Nuclear Journey

Year	*Event*
1955	DPRK scientists attend Nuclear Energy Conference in Moscow
1959	Soviet Union and DPRK sign agreement on nuclear research and "The Furniture Factory" is built.
1963	Soviet Union Ambassador to DPRK argues against keeping nuclear scientists in DPRK.
1964	After PRC tests nuclear device, DPRK asks PRC for help in building the bomb.
1965	Soviet Union sets up a research reactor at Yongbyon.
1967	Soviet Union refuses to set up nuclear power plant.
1967	DPRK sends a delegation to East Germany to ask for nuclear technology.
1975	DPRK asks PRC for tactical nuclear weapons.
1976	DPRK again asks Soviet Union for a nuclear power plant
1979	DPRK asks for help from Czechoslovakia.
1980	DPRK decides to go solo in developing the bomb
1982	United States spots DPRK developing a 30 megawatt reactor
1985	DPRK signs NPT in exchange for Soviet Power Reactor.
1992	DPRK ratifies the safeguard agreement and agrees to IAEA checks.
1994	Jimmy Carter visits DPRK to negotiate with Kim Il Sung
1994	DPRK signs framework agreement and agrees to halt operations at its nuclear sites.
1998	USA detects underground testing facility.
2002	USA adds DPRK to "axis of evil" that leads to the breakdown of 'Framework agreement'.
2003	Six-Party Talks on denuclearization of DPRK starts.
2005	DPRK agrees to denuclearization in Six-Party Talks
2005	The USA detects a tunnel to be used for nuclear testing
2005	The USA imposes sanctions and DPRK threatens a nuclear test
2006	DPRK conducts first nuclear test with a yield of less than 1 kiloton.
2007	Six-Party Talks reaches an agreement for DPRK to halt plutonium program.
2009	Six-Party Talks end.
2013	DPRK conducts nuclear test
2016	DPRK conducts two nuclear tests
2017	DPRK conducts another nuclear test with a yield of 100 kilotons.
2018	**Singapore Summit** between USA and DPRK. DPRK agrees to denuclearization in exchange for security guarantees.
2019	**Hanoi Summit:** Talks reach a dead end and cancelled after two days
2019	**DMZ Summit** between RoK, DPRK, and USA. USA and DPRK announce resumption of 'nuclear talks'.

Index

*